ZAMBIA
in Pictures

Bella Waters

TF CB
Twenty-First Century Books

Contents

INTRODUCTION — 4

THE LAND — 8

▶ Terrain. Rivers and Lakes. Climate. Flora. Fauna. Natural Resources. Environmental Problems. Cities.

HISTORY AND GOVERNMENT — 20

▶ The Iron Age. European Inroads. Land Grab. Copper Colony. Wind of Change. A New Dawn. Fits and Starts. Government.

THE PEOPLE — 34

▶ Language Groups. Rural and Urban Life. Health Issues. The Scourge of AIDS. Education.

Website address: www.lernerbooks.com

Twenty-First Century Books
A division of Lerner Publishing Group, Inc.
241 First Avenue North
Minneapolis, MN 55401 U.S.A.

web enhanced @ www.vgsbooks.com

CULTURAL LIFE   44

▶ Literature. Religion. Holidays and Festivals.
Music and Dance. Crafts and Fine Art. Food.
Sports and Recreation.

THE ECONOMY   56

▶ Services. Industry. Agriculture. The Informal
Sector. Transportation. Communications. The
Future.

FOR MORE INFORMATION

▶ Timeline   66
▶ Fast Facts   68
▶ Currency   68
▶ Flag   69
▶ National Anthem   69
▶ Famous People   70
▶ Sights to See   72
▶ Glossary   73
▶ Selected Bibliography   74
▶ Further Reading and Websites   76
▶ Index   78

Library of Congress Cataloging-in-Publication Data

Waters, Bella.
    Zambia in pictures / by Bella Waters.
        p.   cm. — (Visual geography series)
    Includes bibliographical references and index.
    ISBN 978-1-57505-955-6 (lib. bdg. : alk. paper)
    1. Zambia—Pictorial works—Juvenile literature. 2. Zambia—Juvenile literature. I. Title.
DT3046.W38 2009
    968.94—dc22   2008014148

Manufactured in the United States of America
1 2 3 4 5 6 – BP – 14 13 12 11 10 09

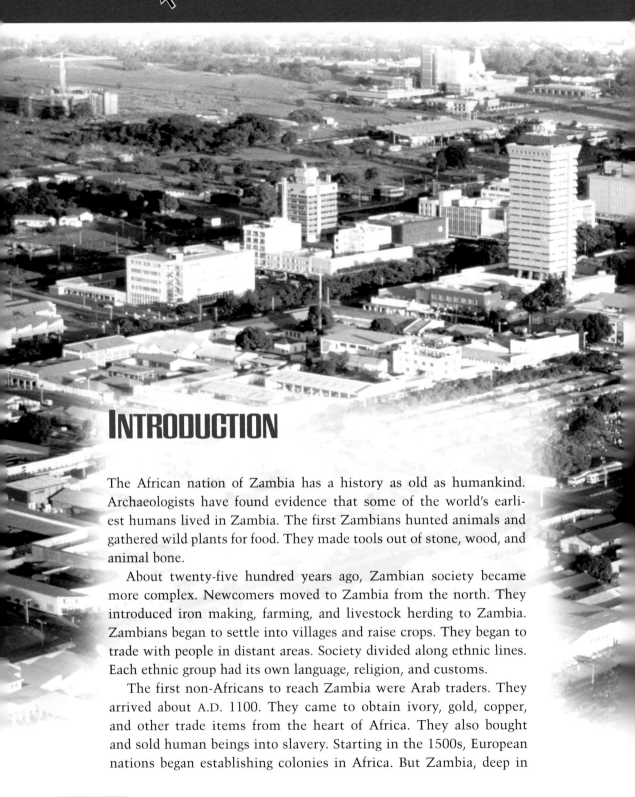

INTRODUCTION

The African nation of Zambia has a history as old as humankind. Archaeologists have found evidence that some of the world's earliest humans lived in Zambia. The first Zambians hunted animals and gathered wild plants for food. They made tools out of stone, wood, and animal bone.

About twenty-five hundred years ago, Zambian society became more complex. Newcomers moved to Zambia from the north. They introduced iron making, farming, and livestock herding to Zambia. Zambians began to settle into villages and raise crops. They began to trade with people in distant areas. Society divided along ethnic lines. Each ethnic group had its own language, religion, and customs.

The first non-Africans to reach Zambia were Arab traders. They arrived about A.D. 1100. They came to obtain ivory, gold, copper, and other trade items from the heart of Africa. They also bought and sold human beings into slavery. Starting in the 1500s, European nations began establishing colonies in Africa. But Zambia, deep in

the African interior, was hard to reach. In the 1800s, British travelers finally arrived in Zambia. In 1889 British businessman Cecil Rhodes claimed Zambia as a British territory.

In the late 1920s, the British realized that Zambia had large deposits of copper. British and other foreign companies began mining operations. Thousands of Zambians took jobs in the copper mines.

The British introduced many of their own customs and traditions to Zambia. They introduced English, which became the nation's official language. They also introduced Christianity, which gradually attracted many Zambian followers. Under British rule, indigenous (native) Zambians suffered greatly. The British took the best land for themselves. They ran the farms, the mines, and the government. Indigenous Zambians were not even allowed to vote.

By the mid-twentieth century, indigenous Zambians were ready to fight back. They wanted independence from Britain. They wanted to choose their own leaders and run their own nation. They organized

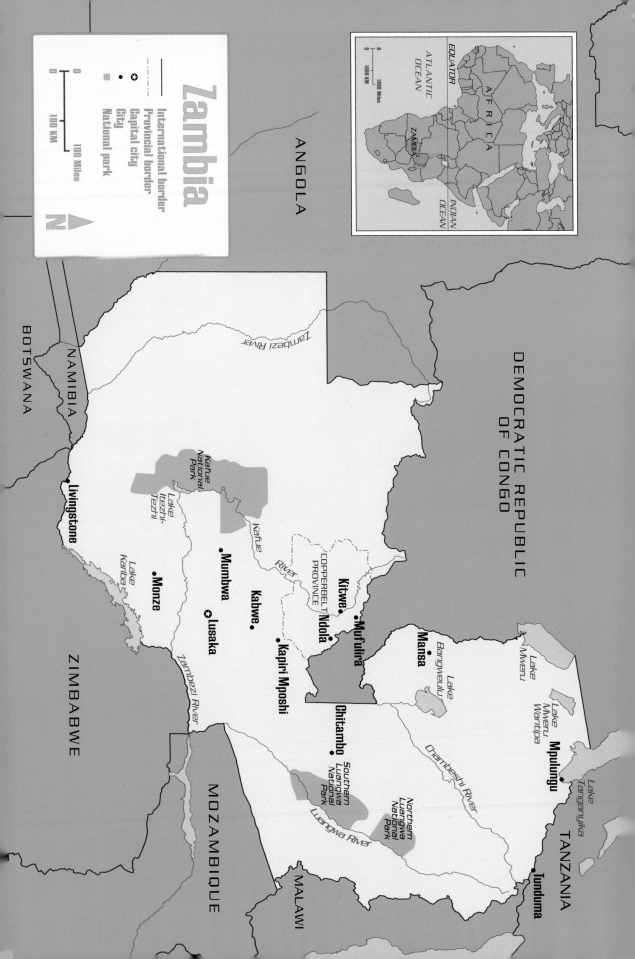

politically and eventually achieved success. In 1964 Zambia became an independent republic.

After independence, Zambia improved its economy, schools, and transportation systems. But when the price of copper fell in the 1970s, the nation's economy also plummeted. In the mid-1980s, Zambia suffered another blow. The acquired immunodeficiency syndrome (AIDS) epidemic hit Zambia and other African nations hard. Zambians began to die by the thousands. Making matters worse, Zambia's president, Kenneth Kaunda, kept gathering more and more power into his own hands.

In 1991 Zambians held new elections and ousted Kaunda from office. Under a new president, Zambia struggled to improve its economy. But most people were crushingly poor. AIDS and other diseases continued to ravage the population. Many people did not have enough food to eat.

In the 2000s, Zambia is home to about 11.5 million people. It is one of the world's poorest nations, but it also has many strengths. It has a rich culture, with traditions, crafts, and stories dating back thousands of years. It has a creative pool of musicians, artists, and writers—some of whom display their talents on the world stage. Zambia has nineteen national parks and a magnificent array of wildlife, including lions, leopards, zebras, and elephants. Victoria Falls, in southern Zambia, is considered one of the world's seven natural wonders. Every year, hundreds of thousands of tourists come to Zambia to visit the falls, the national parks, and Zambia's other natural attractions.

Zambia is rich in minerals—not only copper but also cobalt, coal, silver, gold, uranium, and gemstones. The mining industry provides jobs for thousands of Zambians and brings money into the nation's treasury. In 2006 energy experts discovered oil and gas reserves in Zambia. These resources could be another source of income for Zambia.

The fish eagle is Zambia's national bird. It appears on the nation's flag, where it symbolizes the people's ability to rise above their problems. Indeed, Zambia has many problems. But like the fish eagle, the Zambian people are determined to soar above them.

THE LAND

Zambia is a landlocked country, meaning it is completely surrounded by land, with no borders on an ocean or sea. With 290,585 square miles (752,615 square kilometers) of land, it is a little larger than the U.S. state of Texas.

Zambia is shaped a little like a butterfly, with a big "wing" in the southwest and a smaller "wing" in the northeast. A narrow section of the Democratic Republic of Congo (DRC) drops down between the two wings.

The DRC and Tanzania border Zambia to the north. Malawi and Mozambique sit along its eastern border. Its southern neighbors are Zimbabwe, Botswana, and Namibia. Angola is to the west.

◉ Terrain

Zambia sits on a vast plateau, or high plain, that covers much of central and southern Africa. In the west and southwest, Zambia is mostly flat, with some rolling hills and river valleys. The highest areas in this region are the Tonga Plateau and the Zambezi Escarpment (a kind of cliff) in the south and the Kayamba Hills in the north. In between, swamps, plains, and river valleys dot the land.

Eastern Zambia has several highland areas. The Mbala Highlands and the Mafinga Hills are near the Tanzania–Malawi border. The Muchinga Mountains lie in the southeast. The Mufulwe Hills sit near the tail end of the DRC. The east also has many swamps and river valleys.

Most of Zambia is between 3,000 and 4,500 feet (914 and 1,371 meters) above sea level. The mountains and highlands rise to higher elevations, while the swamps and river valleys have lower elevations. The highest point in Zambia is an unnamed peak in the Mafinga Hills. It measures 7,549 feet (2,301 m) above sea level.

Rivers and Lakes

A network of rivers and streams crisscrosses Zambia, although some of the rivers are dry part of the year. The major rivers are the Kafue in Central

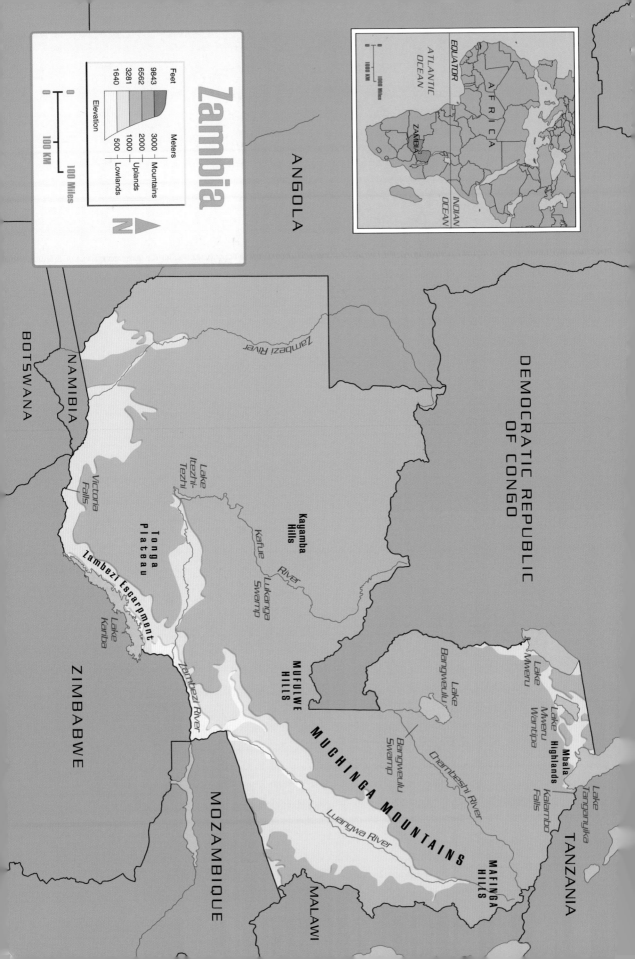

Zambia

Elevation

Feet	Meters	
9843	3000	Mountains
6562	2000	
3281	1000	Uplands
1640	500	
		Lowlands

0   100 KM

0   100 Miles

N

ATLANTIC OCEAN

EQUATOR

AFRICA

ZAMBIA

INDIAN OCEAN

0   1000 Miles

0   1000 KM

ANGOLA

DEMOCRATIC REPUBLIC OF CONGO

TANZANIA

MALAWI

MOZAMBIQUE

ZIMBABWE

BOTSWANA

NAMIBIA

Zambezi River

Victoria Falls

Zambezi Escarpment

Lake Kariba

Zambezi River

Tonga Plateau

Lake Itezhi-Tezhi

Kafue River

Lukanga Swamp

Kayamba Hills

MUFULWE HILLS

MUCHINGA MOUNTAINS

Luangwa River

Chambeshi River

Bangweulu Swamp

Lake Bangweulu

Lake Mweru

Lake Mweru Wantipa

Mbala Highlands

Kalambo Falls

Lake Tanganyika

MAFINGA HILLS

Zambia, the Luangwa in the southeast, and the Chambeshi in the northeast. The Zambezi flows through western Zambia then turns eastward to create Zambia's southern border with Botswana, Namibia, and Zimbabwe. Zambia's rivers provide water for drinking, washing, farming, and recreation. On some of the rivers, people have built dams that generate electricity.

In many places, the rivers drop over high cliffs, creating spectacular waterfalls. The most famous of these waterfalls is Victoria Falls, located on the Zambezi near the city of Livingstone. The Zambezi is about 1 mile (1.6 km) wide when it hits the falls. Suddenly, it plunges 355 feet (108 m) into a narrow, twisting canyon, creating a dramatic roar, mist, and spray.

GREAT RIVER

Zambezi means "great river" in the Tonga language, which is spoken by people in the Victoria Falls region of Zambia. The river is the fourth-longest in Africa, behind the Nile, the Congo, and the Niger. It begins in northwestern Zambia and travels 1,700 miles (2,735 km) before finally emptying into the Indian Ocean. Along the way, it loops through the eastern edge of Angola, forms the Zambia–Zimbabwe border, and cuts across Mozambique.

Victoria Falls is the result of the Zambezi River plunging over a cliff into a narrow gorge on the border of Zambia and Zimbabwe.

"SMOKE THAT THUNDERS"

Victoria Falls is on a list called the Seven Natural Wonders of the World. This list includes other awe-inspiring natural places, such as Mount Everest, the world's tallest mountain, and the enormous Grand Canyon in the United States. Long before Europeans arrived in Africa, local people had their own names for the falls. The Makololo people called them Mosi oa Tunya. This name means "smoke that thunders." It refers to the giant cloud of mist and spray (smoke) created by the falls and the loud roar (thunder) of the water as it pours into the narrow canyon below. Sunlight shining through mist creates dramatic rainbows above the water, and the Tokaleya people called the falls Shongwe, which means "rainbow" in their language. In 1855 explorer David Livingstone became the first European to see the falls. He renamed them for Queen Victoria—ruler of the British Empire at the time.

Zambia has several large lakes. Lake Mweru crosses the border with the DRC, in the northwest of Zambia's eastern section. Lake Tanganyika, the world's longest freshwater lake, forms the border between the DRC and Tanzania. The lake's southernmost tip reaches into northern Zambia. Between Lake Mweru and Lake Tanganyika, Lake Mweru Wantipa sits entirely within Zambia. Lake Bangweulu is located directly south of Mweru Wantipa, east of the city of Mansa.

Lake Kariba is a human-made lake. It straddles the Zambia–Zimbabwe border to the east of Victoria Falls. The lake was created in 1958, when engineers dammed the Zambezi to generate hydroelectric power. With an area of 2,000 square miles (5,180 sq. km), Lake Kariba is one of the largest artifical lakes in the world. Lake Itezhi-Tezhi is also a human-made lake, created by the damming of the Kafue River in 1976. This lake borders Kafue National Park.

Zambia has many swamplands—wet, low-lying areas near lakes and rivers. The Bangweulu Swamp is a large swamp around Lake Bangweulu. The Lukanga Swamp sits in central Zambia, between the cities of Mumbwa and Kabwe. Other swamps are found around Lake Mweru Wantipa and along the Kafue River.

Climate

Zambia is located south of the equator, an imaginary line that divides Earth into Northern and Southern hemispheres, or sections. Most places near the equator, including Zambia, have year-round warm weather.

The hottest months in Zambia are September, October, and November, when daily high temperatures average 86°F (30°C). The coldest months are May through August, with average daily high temperatures of 75°F (24°C). But temperatures can be much higher or lower, depending on elevation. In low-lying areas, temperatures often soar to 100°F (38°C) in October. In highland regions, temperatures can dip under 45°F (7°C) in June and July.

November through March is the rainy season in Zambia. January is the rainiest month, with an average of 9 inches (23 centimeters) of rainfall. Total rainfall ranges from 27 inches (69 cm) per year in the capital city of Lusaka to 52 inches (132 cm) per year in the city of Ndola. The heavy rains flood low-lying grasslands, turn dry streambeds into raging torrents, and turn dusty roads into rivers of mud. Farmers rely on the life-giving rains, but the rain can also be deadly. With the rain come swarms of mosquitoes, which transmit deadly diseases such as malaria.

During the **rainy season,** Zambia's dirt roads become difficult to travel.

The dry season begins in April and stretches into October. During this period, almost no rain falls. The land turns dry and dusty. This is the time when farmers harvest their crops and prepare for the next growing season. The air is generally cool from April to August and grows blistering hot in September and October. So when the wet season finally arrives in November, people are desperate for rain.

Flora

Woodlands cover most of Zambia. These areas are filled with small trees, bushes, and grasses, with lots of open space between the trees. Mopane trees are common in the Zambian woodlands. These small trees are also called butterfly trees because of the shape of their leaves. Other woodland trees include bulging baobab trees and thorny acacia trees.

Denser forestlands cover a few areas of Zambia. The southwest has forests of Zambezi teak, tall trees whose wood is prized for making furniture. Ebony, mango, bamboo, banana, palm, gardenia, fig, and mahogany trees grow along the banks of Zambia's rivers. Evergreen trees grow on mountain slopes. Zambia's swamplands are filled with papyrus and other water-loving plants.

This forest of **mopane trees** stands in one of Zambia's national parks.

Some parts of Zambia are open grasslands, blanketed by grasses, herbs, and wildflowers such as orchids. Some grasslands sit high on mountain slopes. Others spread along the edges of rivers, streams, and lakes.

⊙ Fauna

Animals of many varieties make their homes in Zambia. Big mammals include lions, leopards, cheetahs, and smaller cats; hyenas and wild dogs; and baboons, monkeys, and other primates. Antelopes, including waterbucks, wildebeests, elands, and impalas, live in Zambia. Elephants, rhinoceroses, hippopotamuses, African buffalo, zebras, and giraffes live here too. Small mammals include mongooses, otters, honey badgers, aardvarks, porcupines, hares, and squirrels.

More than 750 species of birds live in Zambia. Among the most unusual are the big blue shoebill stork and the red, white, and black Chaplin's barbet. Eagles, hawks, vultures, buzzards, cuckoos, parrots, owls, swallows, kingfishers, hornbills, cranes, warblers, and woodpeckers are more common bird types.

Zambia's rivers and lakes hold more than four hundred species of fish, including catfish, salmon, tilapia, bream, Nile perch, and tiger fish. Frogs and other amphibians make their homes in and around Zambia's waters. Crocodiles live in the rivers, lakes, and swamps.

Big monitor lizards—which can be more than 4 feet (1.2 m) long—live around Zambia's rivers and swamps. Snakes slither through riverbanks, tall grasses, and forests. Black mambas, puff adders, vipers, and spitting cobras are among the most venomous of these snakes. More than one thousand

ZAMBIA'S BIRD

The African fish eagle *(below)* is Zambia's national bird. It lives near rivers and lakes and feeds on fish. This bird can turn its head far back over its shoulder. It has a loud, shrill call. A picture of an African fish eagle appears on Zambia's flag.

TERMITE TOWERS

Zambia is home to many termites. These small insects are common in warm places. It's easy to see where termites live. Termites build nests out of soil mixed with saliva. These nests take the form of mounds that can be 20 feet (6 m) high. Inside the mounds, the termites live in chambers and tunnels. It's common to see tall termite mounds in the Zambian countryside. Often, vines and other plants grow around the mounds, covering them with leaves and branches.

species of butterflies live in Zambia. Many insects, including mosquitoes and tsetse flies, carry dangerous diseases.

◉ Natural Resources

Zambia is rich in mineral resources. It is one of the world's largest copper producers, with about 10 percent of the world's copper reserves. Most of the copper mines are in north central Zambia. In fact, Copperbelt is the name of the province that contains most of the copper deposits. In addition to copper, Zambia also has deposits of zinc, lead, uranium, cobalt, coal, gold, silver, and emeralds.

Zambia has turned its many rivers into a natural resource. It has

A supervisor watches as workers operate machinery at a copper mine.

built hydroelectric plants on the Kafue, the Zambezi, and other rivers. These plants use the power of rushing water to generate electricity. Zambia uses the electric power for its own needs and exports some of the power to nearby nations.

About 7 percent of Zambia's land is suitable for farming. People grow corn, rice, peanuts, flowers, fruits, vegetables, and other crops on small plots of land. People also raise cattle, goats, pigs, and chickens.

Environmental Problems

Like every nation on Earth, Zambia suffers from a number of environmental problems. In cities, factories and refineries pollute both the air and water. Many water supplies in Zambia are contaminated with bacteria that cause disease.

Mining causes much environmental damage. The mining of copper, lead, and other minerals pollutes the soil, air, and rivers with toxic (poisonous) metals. Mines also scar the landscape. Before digging for minerals, miners use heavy equipment to clear the land of trees and plants. Animals can no longer make their homes there. Without tree roots, the soil around mines becomes loose. It washes away in the rain—a process called erosion.

In some areas, farmers use a technique called slash-and-burn agriculture. To clear fields for growing crops, they cut down trees and plants in wilderness areas (the "slash" part of the process). Then they burn the fallen trees and plants, leaving the land clear for plowing. The soil remains fertile for a few years, but then farmers must move on and clear new areas. When practiced across a large region, slash-and-burn agriculture damages the delicate balance of nature. Wild plants and animals can no longer make their homes in the cleared fields. As with mining, the soil becomes loose and washes away in the rain.

People in Zambia cut down trees for other reasons. People need wood to build homes and to burn for fuel. Woods such as teak and mahogany are especially valuable, so loggers cut down these trees in large numbers. People also cut down trees to make room for roads, buildings, and other structures. Many once-dense forests in Zambia have become thin and bare.

LEAN YEARS

In the early years of the 2000s, Zambia experienced severe droughts. The winter rains fell far short of normal levels. Without enough water, crops failed and farm animals died. People went hungry. Zambia had to ask for food donations from other countries. When rains are plentiful, Zambia can grow enough food for its own people, with some left over to sell to neighboring countries.

Hunting has greatly damaged Zambian wildlife. People in Zambia hunt large animals for food and for sport. They also hunt animals to sell their skins and horns. As a result, certain species have dwindled in numbers or died out altogether. For instance, only small numbers of elephants remain in Zambia. Black rhinoceroses have all been killed off in Zambia. Crocodiles in Zambia are threatened, or in danger of dying out altogether. The Zambian government has passed laws against poaching (illegal hunting), but many poachers go uncaught and unpunished.

To protect its plants and animals, Zambia has established nineteen national parks. The largest is Kafue National Park, which covers more than 8,600 square miles (22,274 sq. km) in western Zambia. Other large parks are the Northern Luangwa National Park and the Southern Luangwa National Park, which stretch along the Luangwa River in eastern Zambia. Tourists come to Zambia from all over the world to tour the national parks and photograph the wildlife in its natural state. The parks are off-limits to hunters, loggers, farmers, and builders.

Visit www.vgsbooks.com for links to websites with additional information about the threats to the environment in Zambia, as well as links to websites about Zambia's national parks and wildlife.

Cities

About 40 percent of Zambians live in urban areas. Lusaka is the capital city. It is home to about one million people—almost 10 percent of the nation's population. Lusaka is located in south central Zambia. It is about halfway between Ndola in the north and Livingstone in the south.

Lusaka was once a small indigenous village. When the British arrived in the late nineteenth century, they used Lusaka as a headquarters from which to administer their new territory. In 1935 the British chose Lusaka as the colony's capital city. In the mid-twentieth century, the movement for Zambian independence was centered in Lusaka.

In modern times, Lusaka is a bustling capital city. It is home to an international airport, the University of Zambia, restaurants, parks, and museums. It sits along the major roads and railroad lines that link the big cities of southern and central Africa.

NDOLA (population 375,000) is the heart of the Copperbelt Province and the second-largest city in Zambia. It was once a small village

Cairo Road is one of the main streets through **Lusaka.**

and a center for slave trading and small-scale copper mining. In the early twentieth century, foreign companies started to mine the copper deposits on a major scale. Workers poured into Ndola and nearby cities to take jobs in the copper mines. Modern Ndola has copper refineries and other industrial businesses. It also has shops, restaurants, and other urban attractions.

KITWE is slightly smaller than Ndola, with a population of about 360,000. It too is a copper mining town. Pit mines and mine tailings (piles of waste minerals from the mines) sit not far from the city center. Kitwe has little to offer in the way of nightlife or cultural attractions. It is mostly an industrial area, with residences for mine workers and their families.

LIVINGSTONE (population 100,000) is primarily a jumping-off point for tourists visiting nearby Victoria Falls. The city is named for explorer David Livingstone, the first European to see the falls. It served as the capital of British-held Zambia from 1911 to 1935. The modern city still has many buildings from British colonial times. It also has shops, hotels, and restaurants catering to tourists.

HISTORY AND GOVERNMENT

Humans have lived in Zambia for hundreds of thousands—maybe even millions—of years. At several sites in Zambia, archaeologists have found stone tools dating back more than 200,000 years. The people who created these tools were probably *Homo erectus*, an early type of human being. Archaeologists have also found bones and tools from a being called Broken Hill Man. He lived between 125,000 and 300,000 years ago. Scientists aren't sure whether Broken Hill Man belonged to *Homo erectus* or another early human species.

After *Homo erectus*, a species called *Homo sapiens* emerged in Africa. These were the first modern human beings. They made tools out of stone, used fire for cooking and heating, hunted large animals, and gathered wild plants for food. Scientists have found stone axes, grinding stones, and other evidence showing that early *Homo sapiens* lived in Zambia more than one hundred thousand years ago.

The term *Stone Age* refers to the era in which people primarily used stone to make tools. In southern and central Africa, the Stone

Age began with the emergence of the first humans and lasted until the early centuries B.C. During this period, Africans developed new skills and created new kinds of tools. They developed languages, created artwork, and invented weapons such as bows and arrows. In addition to stone, people made tools and weapons from wood and animal bone.

Stone Age Zambians probably lived in small family groups. They got their food by hunting and gathering. They used wood, reeds, and grasses to build simple houses. They also used caves as shelters. At several sites in Zambia, caves are filled with Stone Age paintings. Some paintings show elephants, antelopes, and human hunters with spears. Others are simple geometric designs. The artists probably used powdered minerals, animal fats, and dyes from plants to make the paint.

The Iron Age

About twenty-five hundred years ago, people began to migrate into Zambia from the north. These people knew how to make tools

BROKEN HILL MAN

In 1921 Zambian miners digging for zinc and lead discovered a skull *(below)*, bones, and stone tools dating to the Stone Age. The find was near the city of Kabwe, which is also known as Broken Hill. So scientists called the skeleton Broken Hill Man. Archaeologists determined that the bones were between 125,000 and 300,000 years old. The skull has traits common to *Homo erectus*, one of the ancestors of modern human beings. But scientists aren't sure whether Broken Hill Man was a member of *Homo erectus* or another prehuman species.

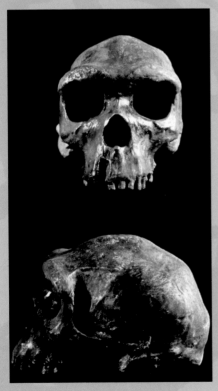

out of iron. Their arrival marked the beginning of the Iron Age in Zambia. The newcomers were farmers and herders—people who raised livestock. They also used clay to make pottery.

With the arrival of these new technologies, Zambian culture became more complex. People settled into villages and planted crops. Iron axes made it easier to cut down trees, so people could clear large amounts of land for farming. Animals such as cattle provided them with milk, meat, and skins. Meanwhile, the old Stone Age hunter-gatherers either adopted the new style of living or retreated far into the forest.

People in different Zambian villages began to trade with one another. Trade items included gold, iron, salt, pottery, food, and ivory (which comes from the tusks of elephants and some other animals). Over the centuries, long-distance trade networks developed. By the A.D. 1100s, Zambians were trading with people as far away as the Indian Ocean coast. Some of the traders were Arabs, who crossed the Indian Ocean looking for gold, ivory, and other valuable goods from Africa. They were also interested in trading humans as slaves. In the 1500s, Portuguese merchants (the first Europeans to travel to Africa) joined the far-flung trading network. Traders traveled overland and also by river.

Zambian culture continued to grow more complex. Iron Age Zambians mined copper, which they molded into jewelry, medallions, and

This nineteenth-century engraving shows **Arab traders** transporting slaves.

other objects. They spun cotton to make cloth. They also practiced complicated religions. They worshipped the spirits of their ancestors as well as spirits in nature. They believed that certain people used magic to do harm, while others used magic to heal illness. Men typically married more than one woman. This practice allowed men to father many children, which in turn increased their standing in the community.

For protection from outsiders, Iron Age Zambians chose chiefs, formed armies, and made alliances with neighboring peoples. People divided along ethnic lines. They bonded with neighboring groups based on ties of language, marriage, family, and lifestyle. Some groups conquered nearby peoples to create large kingdoms. Big kingdoms were often divided into smaller political groups, with local chiefs vying for power.

At some sites in Zambia, archaeologists have found royal graves (tombs for chiefs) from the Iron Age. Chiefs were often buried with signs of their wealth and power, such as gold beads, copper bars, and iron bells.

⊙ European Inroads

Starting in the 1500s, people from European nations—the Portuguese, the British, the Dutch, the Germans, and the French—began to explore and set up colonies throughout Africa. The Europeans were eager to exploit the riches of Africa, including timber, gold, and ivory. But exploring Africa's interior was treacherous. Rivers such as the Zambezi were filled with tall waterfalls, which prevented long-distance travel by boat. Travelers had to struggle through thick jungles, teeming with snakes, spiders, and disease-bearing insects. Only small numbers of outsiders, mostly Arab and Portuguese traders, made it inland as far as Zambia.

Meanwhile, the Zambian kingdoms continued to fight among themselves. Some fought with spears, bows and arrows, and other traditional weapons. But some groups traded with foreigners for powerful new weapons—firearms—which gave them a big advantage in warfare.

Portuguese and Arab traders continued to deal in Zambian copper, ivory, and gold. Traders especially wanted slaves—human captives who brought good prices at slave markets. Zambian chiefs often raided enemy villages and sold conquered men, women, and children to the slave traders. The slave trade moved in two directions. From eastern Zambia, traders took captives to the Indian Ocean coast and then to Middle Eastern slave markets. From western Zambia, traders took slaves to the Atlantic Ocean and then to slave markets in the Americas.

In Great Britain, many people were repelled by slavery. In the late 1700s, British religious leaders began to preach against the African slave trade. Some of these same abolitionists (people who oppose slavery) thought that Africans were backward and savage. Worst of all, the British believed, Africans were pagans—because they practiced traditional religions instead of Christianity. Hand in hand with the antislavery movement, British and other European missionaries (religious teachers) started traveling to Africa. Their goal was to convert Africans to Christianity and to introduce them to European ways.

The most famous of the British missionaries was David Livingstone. He traveled through Zambia during a series of journeys in the 1850s, 1860s, and 1870s. Although he converted very few

David Livingstone

Africans to Christianity, he did earn fame as an explorer. Livingstone's explorations paved the way for more Europeans—missionaries, explorers, traders, and soldiers—to enter the African interior.

Land Grab

Cecil Rhodes, a British businessman and politician, was determined to conquer as much of Africa as possible. In the 1880s, Rhodes made a fortune by buying up diamond mines in the British Cape Colony (modern-day South Africa). He later became prime minister of the Cape Colony. Rhodes knew that the African interior was rich with additional minerals, including gold and copper. He created the British South Africa Company (BSAC) to take over lands north of the Cape Colony for the British Empire.

Rhodes used small groups of soldiers to conquer some territories. But mostly he used trickery. Working through language interpreters, he persuaded African chiefs to sign treaties. The treaties were vague and complicated. The chiefs didn't realize that by signing them, they were handing over their kingdoms to Rhodes. By 1889 Rhodes and the BSAC had taken control of modern-day Zimbabwe and Zambia. Rhodes named these territories Southern Rhodesia and Northern Rhodesia, in his own honor.

Cecil Rhodes relaxes on his porch in South Africa. Rhodes took over much of southern Africa, including Zambia, for the British Empire.

The BSAC set up colonial governments and encouraged British settlers to move to the new territories. At first, the company focused more on Southern Rhodesia (Zimbabwe) than on Northern Rhodesia (Zambia). Southern Rhodesia was rich in gold and easier to reach than remote Northern Rhodesia. Only a small number of British farmers, missionaries, soldiers, and merchants settled in Northern Rhodesia.

To make money from Northern Rhodesia, the BSAC taxed the indigenous people. All adult men had to pay a hut tax (a tax on their homes). The new government shot, imprisoned, or burned the houses of men who refused to pay. Previously, villagers had supported themselves by farming, fishing, and raising animals. All of a sudden, they needed cash to pay their taxes. There was only one to way to get it. Men became migrant laborers. They traveled south on newly built railroad lines to work in the mines of Southern Rhodesia and South Africa. The pay was next to nothing, and the work was brutal. Overseers sometimes beat the workers. By then the British government had outlawed slavery in its African colonies. But the mining system essentially subjected workers to a new kind of slavery.

The shift to migrant labor changed life in indigenous villages. With most of the men gone, women and children carried on as best they could. They continued to farm, fish, and raise animals. But with their family networks broken, the villagers' age-old traditions, religions, and social relationships began to weaken.

Further disrupting village life, more British missionaries arrived in Northern Rhodesia. They opened schools and churches and tried to make indigenous people act more like British Christians. The missionaries denounced indigenous traditions, such as the belief in magic and the practice of men marrying more than one wife.

Under BSAC rule, the people of Northern Rhodesia were considered British subjects. When World War I (1914–1918) began, the British drafted about twenty thousand Northern Rhodesians to work for the British Army in Africa. They worked as military porters (baggage carriers) and manual laborers. Britain also required Northern Rhodesian villages to supply food for British troops. Once the villagers had turned over the required amount of food, they had barely enough left to feed themselves.

Copper Colony

In 1924 the BASC turned over control of Northern Rhodesia to the British Colonial Office. This meant that the British government would rule the nation directly from then on. Under Colonial Office rule, life got even worse for indigenous people. The government set aside the best lands for British farmers only. British settlers voted for members of a lawmaking body called the Legislative Council. Indigenous people were not allowed to vote. They were forbidden to travel and live in certain areas. Essentially, the system worked along racial lines. The British, who were white, enjoyed rights, freedoms, and economic advantages. The indigenous people, who were black, were second-class citizens at best.

By the mid-1920s, only about four thousand British settlers lived in Northern Rhodesia. The indigenous population was more than one million. Small numbers of non-British settlers also lived in Northern Rhodesia. Most of them came from modern-day India and Pakistan. They mostly worked as merchants, setting up shops and other businesses in colonial towns.

HAIL TO THE CHIEF

When the British took over Zambia, they didn't entirely end traditional systems of government. They let indigenous chiefs keep their titles and let them rule on minor local disputes and issues. This system continues into modern times. Especially in the countryside, chiefs play a big role in village government and justice. The position of chief is inherited, meaning it is passed down through either the mother's or the father's side of the family.

Missionaries continued to pressure indigenous people to convert to Christianity. Gradually, their ideas took hold. Although people still practiced traditional religions, groups such as the Watch Tower Bible and Tract Society (Jehovah's Witnesses), the Union Church, and the African Methodist Episcopal Church attracted many indigenous followers.

Indigenous Zambians had been mining small amounts of copper for centuries. But in 1928, the British realized just how large Northern Rhodesia's copper deposits were. The copper rush was on. Big foreign corporations set up copper mining operations in the north. The mines needed a large labor force. Indigenous workers came from all over Northern Rhodesia to take jobs in the mines.

The new copper mining jobs were just as harsh as those in the mines to the south. Men performed backbreaking labor for low pay. Overseers treated them cruelly. All the managers were white, and all the manual laborers were black. Meanwhile, the big companies that owned the mines grew rich selling copper.

Wind of Change

During World War II (1939–1945), Britain again used Northern Rhodesians as military laborers. The price of copper soared during World War II, since armies desperately needed copper for electrical equipment, communications devices, motors, and generators. Northern Rhodesian copper mines prospered during this era.

These **Zambian men are dressed for work in the copper mines.** This photo was taken in the late 1940s.

But by then, the copper miners were fed up with low pay, poor treatment, and racial discrimination. They staged several strikes in the 1930s and 1940s. These work stoppages resulted in only small concessions from management. To better press for change, in the 1940s, workers at each mine banded together into labor unions. In 1949 the individual unions merged into the Northern Rhodesia African Mineworkers Union.

Also in the 1940s, black teachers, clerks, and other skilled workers established groups called welfare associations. The associations fought for indigenous rights. They successfully lobbied the colonial government to allow some blacks to sit on the Legislative Council. In 1948 the associations merged to form the Northern Rhodesian Congress.

Meanwhile, white settlers were unhappy. By the mid-1940s, they made up just 2 percent of the Northern Rhodesian population. They worried that they might lose their power to the black majority. They also felt that Northern Rhodesia wasn't getting its fair share of royalties (regular payments, similar to taxes) from the copper industry. Settlers thought they would fare better economically and politically if Northern Rhodesia were no longer a British colony. They wanted to merge with Southern Rhodesia, which had a bigger white population, and create a new government.

Despite some British opposition, the British government agreed to the settlers' idea. In 1953 Northern Rhodesia, Southern Rhodesia, and the British colony of Nyasaland (modern-day Malawi) joined together to form a state called the Central African Federation.

At first, the new federation prospered. More British settlers arrived, and the copper industry grew. But the federation was troubled. Southern Rhodesians dominated the new government and allocated most of the copper royalties to their own territory. The Colonial Office still controlled some aspects of the government, angering people who wanted complete independence. And indigenous people were not at all happy with the new government, which was still dominated by whites.

In 1958 indigenous leaders formed a new political party, the Zambia African National Congress (ZANC). This group wanted full independence for Northern Rhodesia, with voting rights for everyone—black and white. It also wanted to get rid of the name Northern Rhodesia—which honored the ruthless and racist Cecil Rhodes.

Alarmed by the idea of voting rights for blacks, the federation government banned the ZANC and

THE BRITISH LET GO

Through much of the twentieth century, the British held many colonies in Africa, including modern-day Kenya, Uganda, Burundi, Tanzania, Zambia, Zimbabwe, Botswana, Nigeria, Ghana, and Sierra Leone. The British reaped big profits from businesses in its African colonies. By the 1950s, however, Africans were demanding independence.

In 1960 British prime minister Harold Macmillan argued that it was time to respect Africans' desires for self-rule. In a speech to the South African parliament, he said, "In the twentieth century . . . the processes that gave birth to the nation states of Europe have been repeated all over the world. We have seen the awakening of national consciousness in peoples who have for centuries lived in dependence upon some other power. . . . The wind of change is blowing through [Africa]. . . . We must all accept it as a fact."

Around this time, most of the British colonies declared their independence. The new nations set up democratic governments, with voting rights for all citizens.

—*Rhetoric and Public Affairs*, 2001, http://muse.jhu.edu/demo/ rhetoric_and_public_affairs/ v003/3.4myers.html (May 29, 2008).

imprisoned some of its leaders. So indigenous leaders formed a new party, the United National Independence Party (UNIP).

Nationalism—the movement for self-governance—was not unique to Northern Rhodesia. Across Africa, indigenous people were calling for independence from white, European rule. In the United Kingdom and other European nations, governments saw that they could no longer maintain systems in which a tiny minority ruled a vast majority. A "wind of change" was blowing across Africa, said British prime minister Harold Macmillan in a famous speech in 1960. One by one, African nations began to declare independence from their European colonizers.

The Northern Rhodesian nationalist movement picked up steam and supporters. People united behind the slogan "a new dawn of freedom." In 1962 the British agreed to let Northern Rhodesia rule itself. The Colonial Office held an election for a new national legislature. All adults in Northern Rhodesia were allowed to vote. The UNIP won the election by a big majority. The following year, the Central African Federation dissolved. On October 24, 1964, Zambia

British prime minister **Harold Macmillan** inspects troops in Northern Rhodesia. He favored independence for the colony.

officially became an independent nation, named Zambia after the Zambezi River. Voters chose UNIP leader Kenneth Kaunda as the nation's first president.

▶ A New Dawn

Kenneth Kaunda had a big job on his hands. He governed a nation of people who were mostly uneducated and unskilled. The country was very poor, with large amounts of debt owed to foreign lenders.

Kenneth Kaunda

Kaunda set about to improve the Zambian economy. He raised taxes on the mining industry and used the money to build schools and provide other social services to Zambians. In 1965 the government established the University of Zambia in Lusaka. In 1969 it bought a controlling share in the nation's copper mines, a move that brought even more copper profits into the national treasury.

In the early 1970s, President Kaunda made trade deals with Tanzania to the north east, as well as with the large and powerful Asian nation of China. He worked with China to build roads and railroads from Zambia to Dar es Salaam, the capital of Tanzania. The Zambian government also built several dams to create its own hydroelectric power.

The country was making progress. But in the early 1970s, the price of copper fell dramatically on world markets. As a result, Zambia's copper earnings plummeted, dealing a major blow to the economy. The government had to borrow more money from foreign lenders but was unable to pay back the loans. Rampant inflation, or rising prices, further hurt the economy.

Meanwhile, President Kaunda, by then in his second term, began to take more power into his own hands. He and the UNIP tightened their control of the national government. In 1973 the UNIP-controlled legislature approved a new constitution that made the UNIP the only legal political party in Zambia. In 1975, to smother opposition voices, the party took over Zambia's biggest newspaper.

Kaunda and the UNIP held onto power throughout the 1980s. But Zambians wanted a true democracy. They protested against Kaunda's government and demanded multiparty elections. President Kaunda agreed—perhaps certain that his party would win the elections. But Kaunda was wrong. In elections held in October 1991, a party named the Movement for Multiparty Democracy (MMD) won a large majority of legislative seats. The head of the party was Frederick Chiluba, a trade union leader. He became Zambia's second president.

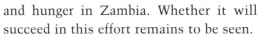

○ Fits and Starts

When Chiluba took office, Zambia's economy was worse than ever. The nation was sinking under the great weight of its foreign debt. Increasing the economic woes, Zambia was hit hard by the AIDS epidemic. By the thousands, Zambians began to grow sick and die. Tens of thousands of children became orphans. The epidemic further weakened Zambian society.

President Chiluba made a variety of economic reforms. He tried to attract foreign investment to Zambia. He welcomed tourists, recognizing that natural wonders such as Victoria Falls could bring large amounts of tourism dollars to Zambia. He worked with international lending agencies, such as the International Monetary Fund and the World Bank, and other foreign groups to shore up the Zambian economy. He also privatized the copper industry. That is, the government sold government-owned copper operations back to private businesses.

Chiluba's efforts had some success, and he won election to a second term as president in 1996. But many people charged that his government was corrupt, with high officials taking bribes and stealing government funds.

In the 2001 elections, MMD won the majority of legislative seats by a narrow margin of victory. A lawyer named Levy Mwanawasa became Zambia's new president. About this time, drought hit Zambia. Harvests were poor, millions were hungry, and the government asked the international community for food aid. The World Bank recognized that Zambia was drowning in debt. In 2005 it brought the nation some economic relief by writing off about half of this debt.

One year later, voters elected President Mwanawasa to a second term in office. His administration is committed to reducing poverty and hunger in Zambia. Whether it will succeed in this effort remains to be seen.

○ Government

Zambia has a democratic government. Citizens elect the president and members of the National Assembly (the national legislature). All citizens aged eighteen and older are eligible to vote.

The president is the head of government and the commander in chief of the armed forces. He or she serves a five-year term, with a two-term limit. The president appoints a cabinet, or group of top advisers,

Levy Mwanawasa

from among members of the National Assembly. The president also appoints the vice president.

The National Assembly has 158 members. Voters elect 150 of these members to five-year terms. (The nation is divided into 150 voting districts, with voters in each one electing a single representative.) The president appoints 8 members, also to five-year terms.

The Zambian judicial system consists of a series of local, regional, and national courts. The Supreme Court is the nation's highest court. It hears appeals of cases from lower courts.

Zambia is divided into nine provinces. The president appoints ministers to govern each province. Provinces are further divided into districts. Voters in each district elect representatives to serve on district councils. The councils oversee matters of district governance. At the city and village level, government leaders include chiefs, community elders, and elected and appointed officials.

 Visit www.vgsbooks.com for links to websites about recent events in Zambia, including news stories and photographs.

THE PEOPLE

Zambia has a population of about 11.5 million. The population density is about 40 people per square mile (15 people per sq. km). This is a low density figure compared to many other African nations. Lusaka and the Copperbelt are the most densely populated areas, while much of the countryside is sparsely populated.

The typical Zambian woman will give birth to five or six children in her lifetime. The population is growing at a rate of 1.9 percent per year. The population is expected to reach about 15 million in the year 2025.

◉ Language Groups

Almost 99 percent of Zambia's people are black Africans, descended from indigenous people of earlier centuries. About 1 percent of Zambians have a European heritage. Most of these Zambians are the descendants of white British colonists. A very small number of Zambians—less than 1 percent—belong to other ethnic groups. Most of these Zambians

are descended from southern Asian (Indian or Pakistani) colonists who arrived in Zambia early in the twentieth century.

Zambians belong to dozens of different ethnic groups. Scholars label these groups according to language. That is, people in Zambia who speak the Tonga language belong to the Tonga ethnic group. Those who speak Bemba belong to the Bemba group, and so forth.

The Bemba is the largest language/ethnic group in Zambia. Most Bemba-speaking people live in north central Zambia—around Copperbelt Province—and in the western section of Zambia's eastern wing. More than 2.25 million Zambians speak Bemba.

Tonga speakers constitute the second-largest language group. Most Tonga speakers live in southern Zambia, in the areas around Livingstone and Lusaka. More than one million Zambians speak Tonga.

The next-largest language group is the Lozi. Lozi speakers are scattered throughout southwestern Zambia. They number more than 500,000. Tumbuka speakers live in eastern Zambia, near the Malawi

DRESSED FOR THE WEST

Most Zambians wear Western-style clothing—that is, they dress a lot like people in North American and Europe. In fact, much of the clothing worn in Zambia comes from the United States. It is mainly used clothing, which Americans have donated to charities. Zambians buy the clothing at outdoor markets.

For Zambian men, T-shirts, button-down shirts, jeans, sandals, and tennis shoes are common items of clothing. Women usually wear Western-style tops, skirts, dresses, and shoes. They are expected to dress modestly, which means no shorts or skirts that expose their legs above the knee.

In earlier eras, Zambian women wore *chitenges*. These were lengths of colorful printed cloth, worn as wraparound skirts, gowns, and head scarves. Some Zambian women still wear chitenges, especially at festivals and other special events. But for day-to-day activities, Western dress is the norm.

border. Their numbers total more than 430,000. About 330,000 Zambians speak Nsenga. Most of them live near the Mozambique border. Mambwe-Lungu speakers, numbering more than 280,000, live in northeastern Zambia. Other large language/ethnic groups are the Kaonde, the Lunda, the Luvale, the Luyana, and the Mbunda.

English is the official language of Zambia. This was the language used by British authorities in the late nineteenth and twentieth century, and it became the language of Zambian business, government, and education. Throughout Zambia, especially in urban areas, many people speak English as well as a local language. In some rural areas, people speak only their ethnic language and no English.

In eastern and central Zambia, many people speak a language called Nyanja. Unlike Bemba, Tonga, and the other ethnic languages, Nyanja is not associated with one ethnic group. Instead, it is a simplified language that people of different groups use to speak with one another. Even though English is the nation's official language, the Zambian police and armed forces use Nyanja as their primary language.

◉ Rural and Urban Life

About 60 percent of Zambians live in rural areas. They make their homes in small villages scattered around the countryside. Like their ancestors, most rural Zambians make their living by farming, fishing, and raising livestock. Many are subsistence farmers. That is, they raise just enough food to feed their families, with little left over to sell. Others have larger farms and sell most of their crops for cash.

Most Zambians live in **villages** like this one. They build their homes out of whatever materials they can gather in the area.

Important food crops include corn, peanuts, beans, potatoes, yams, mangos, bananas, and a starchy root called cassava. Most rural villages have a few shops, a Christian church, and an outdoor market, where vendors sell vegetables, fruit, fish, nuts, and other products.

People in the Zambian countryside live simply. Some build houses out of wooden poles and thatch (a mat of grasses), plastered with mud. Others build houses out of mud bricks, cement blocks, or pieces of sheet metal. Most houses have just one room and windows without glass. Rural people don't own much furniture. They often sit on the floor on bamboo mats.

Many villages do not have electrical power lines. In these places, shop owners use gasoline-powered generators to run refrigerators and other equipment. Some people have battery-operated radios and other appliances. But most rural people make do without electricity. For lighting, they use kerosene lamps. Women usually cook outdoors over small charcoal stoves. Some villages have wells, which provide fresh-water for drinking, cooking, and bathing. In villages without wells, people tote water from nearby rivers and lakes.

Very few people have motor vehicles in rural Zambia. They travel on foot. It's common to see women walking with heavy sacks of nuts or other goods balanced on their heads and herders ushering goats and other animals through the center of town. When people need to travel long distances, they usually take buses.

Urban life is more varied. People in Zambian cities work in a variety of businesses: factories, government offices, mines, stores, restaurants, open-air markets, banks, and schools. Lusaka, Livingstone, and several other cities were once British colonial headquarters. The early British inhabitants built parks, schools, and other buildings that reminded them of their hometowns in Great Britain. In the years since colonial times, city dwellers have built new office towers, shops, and other buildings. City roads are filled with cars, buses, and taxis.

Zambian cities have a mix of rich and poor inhabitants. Wealthy residents live in spacious homes on neat, treelined streets. They enjoy clean water supplies, electricity in their houses, and good sanitation facilities. In contrast, the poorest urban dwellers make their homes in shantytowns. Here, people use scrap metal, wood, and other materials to build ramshackle houses. Life is very difficult in the shantytowns, which don't have electric power lines, indoor toilets, or running water. Many poor city dwellers grow crops in backyard gardens and raise animals for extra food.

These storefronts show the variety of businesses in Zambia's cities. This picture was taken in Kapiri Mposhi.

Most of Zambia's white and southern Asian citizens live in cities. The cities are also home to large groups of refugees from surrounding nations, as well as migrants from the countryside.

Health Issues

On health issues, Zambia is one of the world's most troubled nations. Life expectancy is about 38 years for both men and women. By comparison, life expectancy in the United States is 75 years for men and 80 years for women. In Zambia more than 18 percent of children die before they reach the age of five.

Zambia is a fairly peaceful country. It often serves as a safe haven for people from nearby war-torn nations. For instance, in December 2000, about 60,000 refugees fled to Zambia from the nearby DRC (which was then enduring a civil war). In 2006 international organizations estimated that more than 140,000 foreign refugees were living in Zambia. Many of them live in makeshift camps, set up by international aid agencies. Others live in shantytowns in Zambia's big cities. Zambia has trouble providing food and social services for its own people. The influx of large numbers of refugees taxes the nation even further.

The roots of Zambia's health problems are many. For one thing, more than half of rural Zambians have no access to clean water. Water gathered from lakes, rivers, and even some wells is often contaminated with disease-causing bacteria. The water can make people sick with diarrhea, hepatitis A, typhoid, and cholera.

Malaria is common in Zambia. Each year about 2 million Zambians contract the dangerous and sometimes fatal disease. Malaria spreads through the bite of anopheles mosquitoes. These mosquitoes are thick during Zambia's rainy season. Many young children die of malaria as soon as the rains begin.

In wealthier nations, doctors administer vaccines to protect people from typhoid, hepatitis, and other diseases. They use drugs to treat malaria. They prescribe antibiotics to treat bacterial infections. But Zambia's health-care system is very poor. Many towns have only a small health clinic to care for thousands of people. Clinics are poorly supplied and poorly staffed. They have only small supplies of vaccines, antibiotics, and other drugs. They don't have X-ray machines and other basic medical equipment.

Making matters worse, Zambia suffers from a shortage of health-care professionals. After completing school, many Zambian doctors and nurses leave the nation for jobs in Europe or the United States, where pay is much higher than it is in Zambia. The ratio of patients to doctors in Zambia is 14,000 to 1, compared to about 600 to 1 in Europe and North America. Zambia has only about 17,000 nurses in the entire nation. Because of this shortage, most Zambian women give birth without the help of a doctor, nurse, or trained midwife. The rate of maternal death (the number of mothers who die during or around the time of childbirth) is very high in Zambia.

The problems of poor health care are made worse by hunger. When drought hits Zambia, as it did in the early 2000s, crops fail. People begin to starve. Even in times of good harvest, many families are not able to grow or afford enough food to feed their children. Some Zambian babies are dangerously underweight. Some die of malnutrition. People who are hungry have weakened immune systems. Their bodies are not able to fight off diseases. They are more likely to die of cholera or another illness than are people with good nutrition.

Visit www.vgsbooks.com for links to websites with more information about the people of Zambia.

A woman carries her child and a bag of corn she received from an international aid organization. Droughts in the early 2000s left many Zambians without food.

Women and children await a **mobile (traveling) health clinic** in rural Zambia. Health care in Zambia is difficult to find because of a shortage of clinics and doctors.

The Scourge of AIDS

AIDS is another health crisis in Zambia. AIDS is an often-fatal disease. It is caused by the human immunodeficiency virus (HIV). HIV spreads through blood and other body fluids. It is commonly spread through sex.

International organizations estimate that more than 16 percent of Zambian adults are infected with HIV. This is one of the highest rates of HIV infection in the world. Almost 100,000 Zambians die of AIDS every year. About 700,000 Zambian children are AIDS orphans—with both parents having died of AIDS.

Local and international health organizations are working to prevent AIDS in Zambia and to treat people who have the illness. These efforts are not easy. Many Zambians don't know how to protect themselves from HIV. Many do not use condoms, which can prevent the spread of HIV during sex. Many Zambian men have many sexual partners. They spread HIV to their wives and girlfriends. It's possible for HIV-infected mothers to spread the virus to babies during childbirth. Many Zambian children become infected this way.

In recent years, drug companies have developed life-extending medicines for people with HIV and AIDS. The United States and international organizations have funded programs to distribute these medicines to people in Zambia and other African nations. However, the programs do not reach far enough. Fewer than 25 percent of Zambian people with HIV/AIDS receive any life-prolonging treatment.

GOOD-BYE TO OLD AGE

Since life expectancy is so low in Zambia, it's uncommon to see elderly people there. Just 2.4 percent of the population is 65 years or older. By comparison, 12.6 percent of the U.S. population is aged 65 or older. Young people make up the majority of Zambia's population. More than 45 percent of Zambia's people are under 15. In the United States, only 20 percent of the population is under 15.

AIDS is one reason that life expectancy in Zambia is so low. Before AIDS emerged in the mid-1980s, people in Zambia could expect to live into their fifties. Since AIDS, life expectancy has dropped to 38 years.

◉ Education

The Zambian government offers free primary school education (grades one to seven) for all children. Children are not required to attend primary school, and only about 67 percent do so. The teacher-student ratio is about 1 teacher for every 57 students. English is the main language of instruction, but teachers also use ethnic languages in the classroom to help students who are not proficient in English.

Zambian children attend a school in the Copperbelt. Education in Zambia is free through grade seven, but many children do not attend school.

Families who want to send their children to secondary school (grades eight to twelve) must enroll them in private schools. Private school fees are too high for most Zambian families, so most children do not attend secondary school. (Instead of going to school, many Zambian children work to help support their families.) Most private schools are run by Christian churches.

The University of Zambia is the nation's largest university, with about five thousand students. It offers training in engineering, law, medicine, business, mining, agriculture, and other professions, as well as the liberal arts (such as history and languages). The university is located in Lukasa. It opened in 1966. Other Zambian universities are Copperbelt University in Kitwe and Northrise University in Ndola.

About 70 percent of Zambians are literate, or able to read and write. The rate is about 82 percent for men and about 61 percent for women. Low rates of literacy add to problems of poverty in Zambia. People who cannot read and write are unlikely to get good-paying jobs.

SECOND-CLASS CITIZENS

Zambian women have long been treated poorly. The man is the head of the Zambian household, and his wife is expected to obey him. Some Zambian men physically abuse their wives. Carrying on an age-old tradition, some men marry more than one wife. Fathers typically arrange marriages for their daughters. Many girls marry and start having children in their early teens.

Many Zambians feel that education is not important for girls. Therefore, Zambian schools tend to have more male than female students. At the University of Zambia, about 75 percent of the students are men. Men also dominate Zambian business and government. Of the nation's 158 parliament members, only about 12 percent are women.

The AIDS epidemic has hit Zambian women very hard. Many women and girls have a hard time protecting themselves from HIV. If her husband wants sex, a wife is expected to obey him, even if he has HIV or refuses to use a condom. Desperately poor, some Zambian girls and women must trade sex for money, which also puts them at a high risk for HIV infection.

CULTURAL LIFE

Zambian culture is a mix of indigenous, British colonial, and modern influences. For instance, many Zambians hold ceremonies and festivals that originated hundreds and perhaps even thousands of years ago. They tell stories that have been handed down from generation to generation over many centuries. At the same time, Zambians practice Christianity and speak English, both of which the British introduced to Zambia. Finally, Zambians like reggae music, Hollywood movies, and other pastimes that are common to modern people all over the world.

 Literature

Before Europeans arrived in Zambia, indigenous people did not use writing systems. Instead, they communicated with words and music. They told stories, sang songs, and beat drums to pass along important information. They used folktales to teach important lessons about life and relationships. One traditional Zambian story, "The Hare's

Revenge," tells how a small hare, or rabbit, outwits a big African buffalo who has treated him cruelly. The lesson is that by using their heads, the small can prevail over the big and strong.

Europeans introduced writing to Zambia. Using the Roman alphabet, Europeans wrote down some of Zambia's languages. They created dictionaries and grammar books. Soon some Zambians learned to read and write in their own languages.

British colonial administrators made English the official language of Zambia, even though most people continued to speak local languages. During the colonial years, most indigenous Zambians did not attend school. Those who did learned about English language and literature. A few Zambians began to write stories and novels in their own languages, however.

After independence the Zambian government improved the nation's school system. More people learned to read and write English as well as indigenous languages. More Zambians also wrote literary works.

Newspapers and magazines were written in both English and indigenous languages.

In modern times, several Zambian writers have earned acclaim. One of them is Binwell Sinyangwe. His novel *Quills of Desire* (1993) tells of a young Zambian man who wants to live in Britain but instead must stay in his poverty-stricken homeland. Another novel by Sinyangwe, *A Cowrie of Hope* (2000), tells how a poor Zambian woman struggles to make life better for her daughter. A writer named Monde Sifuniso has earned praise for "Night Thoughts" (2000) and other short stories. She has also edited collections of stories by other African women writers. Malama Katulwende is both a novelist and a poet. His novel *Bitterness* (2005) explores many of the problems plaguing modern Zambia. Singyangwe, Katulwende, and Sifuniso all write in English.

Religion

In the twentieth century, missionaries converted most Zambians to Christianity. In the twenty-first century, approximately 85 percent of Zambians are Christians. Both main branches of Christianity—

The majority of Zambians are **Christians.** This church is in Monze, a city about two hours south of Lusaka.

A **medicine man** uses charms and magic to treat a sick patient.

Catholic and Protestant—operate churches in Zambia. Christian churches also operate many of the nation's schools and social organizations. Worship services are held in English and indigenous languages, depending on the location.

More than 5 percent of Zambians practice Islam, a religion that originated on the Arabian Peninsula. Arab traders introduced Islam to Zambia in the years of the slave trade. During the colonial period, some southern Asian immigrants to Zambia also practiced Islam (people who practice Islam are called Muslims). These immigrants opened mosques (Islamic temples) and converted some Zambians to their faith. In recent years, Muslims from East African nations such as Somalia and Kenya have settled in Zambia, and more Zambians have converted to Islam. A little more than 5 percent of Zambians practice Hinduism. Hinduism is the dominant religion of India. Indian immigrants brought Hinduism to Zambia in the twentieth century. The remaining Zambians (less than 5 percent) are not affiliated with a major religion.

Many Zambians, including many Christians, also practice traditional indigenous religions, just as their ancestors did. They worship the spirits of nature. They believe in magic—used for both good and evil purposes. They believe that certain places, such as waterfalls, are holy and that some animals, such as crocodiles, have special powers. This kind of belief system is called animism. Animist practices vary from group to group and place to place in Zambia. Traditional beliefs are strongest in rural areas. In cities many people no longer practice traditional religions.

◉ Holidays and Festivals

Zambians celebrate religious and nonreligious holidays. The Christian holidays of Christmas and Easter are official holidays in Zambia. Zambians also celebrate New Year's Day (January 1) and Labor Day (May 1), as do people in many other countries.

May 25, Freedom Day, is a holiday in Zambia and many other African nations. On this day, Africans commemorate the creation of the Organization of African Unity (OAU; later called the African Union) in 1963. The OAU was founded to work for independence, peace, prosperity, and unity for African nations.

Some holidays are specific to Zambia. Youth Day takes place on March 9. Heroes Day and Unity Day, held on the first Monday and Tuesday in July, honor those who fought for Zambia's independence and the creation of a united Zambia. Farmers Day is the first Monday in August. Independence Day, October 24, celebrates Zambia's freedom from British rule.

In addition to public holidays, Zambians hold many festivals and ceremonies. Each ethnic group has its own traditions. Some festivals honor important historical events. For instance, each July the Lunda people hold the Umutomboko ceremony. This festival commemorates a historic military campaign, during which the Lunda conquered tribe after tribe on a journey to Zambia. The two-day ceremony features dances, drumming, and colorful costumes. The chief of the Lunda is the center of attention. He covers his body with white powder, dresses in a brightly colored skirt, and dances with a sword. Lots of good food and drink accompany the festivities.

During the rainy season, the Lozi people hold the Ku-omboka ceremony. *Ku-omboka* means "to get out of the water onto dry ground." In earlier eras, when the Zambezi River flooded the surrounding land during the rainy season, the Lozi loaded their belongings into canoes. They paddled from their dry-season village to their wet-season village, which was out of the way of the floodwaters. Although modern Lozi no longer move between the two villages, the Ku-omboka ceremony reenacts the migration. Musicians beat huge drums to call the people together. Ordinary people travel to the dry-season village in canoes. The Lozi chief travels in a black-and-white-striped barge, propelled by paddlers wearing traditional animal-skin costumes. The chief's barge also carries a sculpture of a big black elephant. The ceremony dates back more than three hundred years.

◉ Music and Dance

In earlier eras, Zambians used music and dance as communication. People beat drums to call villagers together. Songs told stories about

During the Lozi celebration of **Ku-omboka,** the chief travels down the Zambezi River in his barge.

history and famous people. Dancers often dressed in masks, colorful headdresses, and fantastical animal costumes. Their dances, too, told stories about people, gods, animals, and the natural world. Music and dance accompanied weddings, funerals, births, harvest festivals, the naming of new chiefs, and other special occasions.

Musicians played—and some still play—a variety of traditional instruments. For instance, the *mbira*, or thumb piano, is a small wooden box or a hollow gourd with a row of metal or wooden keys. Musicians pluck the keys with their thumbs to play a tune. The *silimba* is like a xylophone. It consists of a series of big flat wooden keys, mounted on hollow gourds. Players strike the keys with mallets to create different notes. Drums of all shapes and sizes are common traditional instruments. So are rattles, bells, and flutes.

In modern times, Zambians often play traditional music at special events. At festivals, modern-day Zambians perform ritual dances, just as their ancestors did generations ago. Dancers often pass down their

MAKISHI DANCERS

In western Zambia, several ethnic groups carry on a tradition called the Makishi masquerade. At ceremonies and special events, Makishi dancers *(below)* dress up in fantastical painted masks. Some masks are carved from wood. Others are fashioned out of bark and wicker. Many have big fiber wigs and headdresses attached. In addition to masks, Makishi dancers wear netted bodysuits, along with cloth and fiber skirts, beads, rattles, and other ornaments. Different masks and costumes represent different animals, monsters, clowns, chiefs, ancestors, and spirits. Dancers act out stories about the characters they represent. Originally, Makishi dancers performed only at initiation ceremonies, during which adolescent boys and girls make the transition from childhood to adulthood. In modern times, the dancers still perform at these ceremonies. But they also dance at other events and festivals, including parties and shows for tourists.

colorful masks and costumes from one generation to the next. Some dances are for men only, women only, or children only, depending on the occasion.

Singing is a common part of Christian worship in Zambia. People sing religious songs in both English and indigenous languages. They often accompany songs with hand clapping, dancing, and elaborate vocal harmonies. Some religious songs are call-and-response style, with a lead singer delivering one line of music and a chorus singing a follow-up line.

Modern Zambians also like new musical styles. In Zambian cities, reggae, rap, and rumba are all popular. People listen to live bands at nightclubs, cafés, and other venues. *Kalindula* is a Zambian musical style that emerged in the late twentieth century. It features rhythmic singing, accompanied by jangly guitars and drums. Several modern Zambian musicians have earned fame in Zambia and beyond. One of them is Brian Chilala. His fusion of rock, reggae, and kalindula has won him fans all over the world.

Crafts and Fine Art

In earlier eras, Zambians made everything they needed out of the materials at hand. They wove baskets out of reeds, grasses, palm leaves, and bark. They used dried gourds as containers for food and water. They made clothing from homespun cotton and animal skins. They used pigments from soil, bark, and leaves to make dyes for decorating baskets, clothing, and other items. Craftspeople carved canoes, furniture, walking sticks, and masks out of wood. They used a combination of animal skins, wood, and gourds to make drums and other musical instruments. Potters used clay to make all kinds of watertight vessels. These items were not only useful, they were also beautiful. Craftspeople also made items just for decoration, such as gold and copper jewelry.

In modern times, Zambians no longer need to make household items by hand. They can buy tools, containers, and other ready-made goods at stores and outdoor markets. However, the crafts tradition has not died out in Zambia. Craftspeople still make beautiful baskets, masks, pottery, clothing, and jewelry. Many of these items aren't made for daily use but are instead sold to tourists as souvenirs.

Many tourists bring home traditional-style Zambian masks as souvenirs.

A number of Zambians work in the fine arts, such as painting, printmaking, and sculpture. Groups such as the Zambia National Visual Arts Council organize shows and promote the work of Zambian artists.

Food

In Zambia, food is sometimes hard to come by. Many people rely on the crops they raise themselves in small backyard gardens. They haul in fish from rivers and lakes. They raise livestock such as goats and cattle.

In rural areas, a food called *nshima* provides the basis for breakfast, lunch, and dinner. Nshima is a warm, thick porridge. It is usually made from corn, dried and ground into a fine meal. Zambians usually eat nshima with milk and sugar for breakfast. They eat nshima with sauces and stews for lunch and dinner. It's standard practice to eat nshima without utensils. Diners roll the porridge into bite-sized balls and dip them into the sauce or stew.

A Zambian woman cooks a pot of nshima.

The sauces and stews are where Zambian cooks get creative. *Ifisashi* is a sauce made of greens, peanuts, onions, and tomatoes. Tiger fish with greens is a popular stew. *Tongabezi* is a stew of sweet potatoes, squash, chicken, onions, tomatoes, and spices. Others sauces and stews contain beef, goat, and lamb; and beans, peas, okra, and other vegetables.

In urban areas, diets are more varied. In addition to nshima, people eat rice, pasta, bread, and potatoes, which they can buy at local markets. Some restaurants serve Western-style meals. Others serve Indian food. In between meals, Zambians snack on peanuts, bananas, mangoes, and other fruits. Many Zambians brew their own beer.

A ZAMBIAN RECIPE: IFISASHI

Ifisashi is a favorite sauce, usually eaten with nshima. You could serve it with rice, pasta, or potatoes instead.

1 cup raw peanuts, shelled and skins removed

1½ cups water

2 tomatoes, peeled and chopped

1 onion, chopped

2–3 pounds collard greens or spinach, stems removed, washed, and chopped

Salt to taste

1. Grind, chop, or pound peanuts into a fine powder.
2. In a large saucepan, bring water to a boil.
3. Add peanuts, tomatoes, and onion. Cook on high heat for several minutes, stirring often.
4. Reduce heat to medium. Stir in greens.
5. Cover saucepan. Cook until mixture becomes a thick, buttery sauce (15–20 minutes). Add water if mixture becomes dry or starts to burn. Salt to taste.
6. Serve hot.

Serves 4 to 6

Sports and Recreation

Like people in many parts of the world, Zambians are soccer crazy. Almost every town and city has its own soccer team. Village children sometimes play soccer with homemade balls when no store-bought ball is available. People avidly follow Zambia's national soccer team. It consistently does well in African tournaments, although it does not rank high in world soccer standings. Zambians also like cricket, a sport from Britain that arrived in Zambia in colonial days.

Only a few Zambian athletes have so far excelled on the world stage. In 1996, at the Olympic Games in Atlanta, Georgia, a track athlete named Samuel Matete won a silver medal in the 400-meter men's hurdles. Another Zambian, Madalitso Muthiya, makes his living as a professional golfer. He even competed in the 2006 U.S. Open, one of the most important U.S. golf tournaments. But these athletes are exceptions. Most Zambians can't afford the high-level coaching, training, and equipment needed to win big-name competitions.

Many visitors come to Zambia for adventure sports. They kayak, canoe, and white-water raft on Zambia's rushing rivers. They view Victoria Falls from above from gliders and helicopters, and they parachute out of airplanes. They hike through the national parks with high-tech binoculars and cameras. The visitors are mostly white

Joseph Musonda *(left)* and Felix Katongo *(right)* of the **Zambian national soccer team** battle with Egyptian player Ahmed Fathy during a match in 2008.

Westerners who can afford expensive outdoor gear, guides, and sporting equipment. Very few Zambians can afford adventure sports. When Zambians take to their nation's rivers and lakes, it is usually to fish from canoes and other small boats.

Zambians enjoy inexpensive pastimes. *Isolo* is a popular indigenous game. It is played on a wooden board with twenty-four holes. Players use seeds, pebbles, or bottle tops as the game pieces. The goal is to capture all your opponents' pieces. Zambian girls play a game called *ichiyenga*. Players dig a small hole in the ground and place stones or seeds around the rim. With one hand, a player tosses a larger stone in the air. Before she catches it, she must use the same hand to knock a smaller stone or seed into the hole. The player who makes the fewest mistakes is the winner.

Like people everywhere, Zambians like movies, TV, radio, and recorded music. Because these entertainments rely on electricity, they are more common in urban areas than rural ones. Also like people everywhere, Zambians enjoy socializing in restaurants, nightclubs, and family homes.

 Visit www.vgsbooks.com for links to websites that explore the culture of Zambia. Listen to and watch videos of Zambian musicians, find recipes for Zambian dishes, and see the latest scores of Zambia's soccer team.

THE ECONOMY

Zambia is one of the poorest nations on Earth. More than 75 percent of Zambians live on less than one dollar per day. About 50 percent do not have full-time employment.

The gross domestic product (GDP)—the total value of all goods and services produced in a country in one year—is a common measure of national wealth. Zambia's GDP is about $7.3 billion. This number is extremely low compared to GDP in most other nations.

▶ Services

The service sector accounts for 56 percent of Zambia's GDP. This sector includes banking, insurance, government, sales, communications, education, and other businesses that provide services instead of making products. About 9 percent of Zambians work in service businesses.

Tourism is a growing service business in Zambia. Every year, more than half a million visitors come to Zambia to explore its national parks, Victoria Falls, and other natural wonders. The tourists spend

their money at restaurants, hotels, and adventure travel companies. They contribute about $100 million to the Zambian economy every year. The Zambian government recognizes tourism as a promising source of income and works with private businesses to encourage tourism.

Industry

The industrial sector (mining, manufacturing, and energy) accounts for 26 percent of Zambia's GDP. About 6 percent of the nation's workers hold jobs in this sector.

Zambia is rich in minerals and metals, especially copper. Zambia is the world's fifth-largest copper producer, with 470,500 tons (427,000 metric tons) extracted in 2004. Another important metal is cobalt, which is used to make drill bits, magnets, medical equipment, electronic devices, paints, inks, dyes, and other products. Zambia is the world's largest producer of cobalt, with about 5,500 tons (5,000

ALL THAT GLITTERS

Zambia has big copper and cobalt deposits. But it also has more glittery minerals. The nation is rich in gemstones, including amethysts, aquamarines, emeralds, garnets, diamonds, rubies, and sapphires. It also has deposits of gold and silver.

Mining companies make a lot of money by extracting and selling Zambia's copper, gems, and other minerals all over the world. Ordinary miners, however, do not share in the companies' riches. They work for wages, which are often very low. Mining is also dangerous work. Cave-ins and explosions at mines have taken the lives of many Zambian miners.

metric tons) extracted each year. Besides copper and cobalt, Zambian workers mine silver, gold, uranium, coal, gemstones, and other minerals. Many Zambians work as miners, while others work in plants that process raw minerals into finished products.

In Lusaka and other big cities, many Zambians hold factory jobs. Some factories produce beverages, chemicals, textiles, or fertilizers. Other factories process food. Zambia produces power at several hydroelectric plants. These plants enable Zambia to create electricity for its own use as well as for export to neighboring countries. In 2006 exploration teams discovered reserves of oil and gas in northwestern Zambia. Experts are not yet sure how large the reserves are. If they are large, oil and gas drilling could bring new jobs and income to Zambia.

These Zambians work at a milk and butter processing plant in Lusaka.

Most Zambian **farmers** have very small plots of land and no mechanized equipment. These subsistence farmers struggle to provide for their families.

Agriculture

Most Zambians—85 percent—make a living by farming. However, agriculture (including farming, fishing, and forestry) accounts for only 18 percent of Zambia's GDP. With so many Zambians working as farmers, one might expect agricultural GDP to be larger. However, most Zambians farm only tiny plots of land. They use simple hand-held tools to till the soil. Even in good years, they raise just enough food to feed their families, with little or none left over to sell. In times of drought or flooding, many farm families go hungry.

Small numbers of Zambians run large farming operations, complete with tractors and other mechanized equipment. The principal crops are corn, rice, peanuts, sunflower seeds, flowers, fruits, vegetables, tobacco, cotton, sugarcane, cassava, and coffee. Farmers also raise cattle, goats, pigs, and chickens. Sometimes, Zambian growers sell tobacco, flowers, grain, and cotton to neighboring nations. For the most part, however, farmers do not export their products. They either consume them themselves or sell them to other Zambians.

As with farming, most Zambians fish for subsistence. They catch fish to feed themselves, with little left over to sell. Fishers travel on

These men **fish** in the Bangweulu Swamp.

lakes and rivers in canoes and other small boats. They use traps, nets, and hooks to pull fish from the water. A few Zambians run large-scale fish farms. They raise fish in ponds and tanks. The most common commercial fish is bream. Commercial fishers sell their catches in a variety of forms: dried, smoked, canned, and fresh. They export small amounts of fish to neighboring nations, but most is eaten in Zambia.

Zambia has a small timber industry. In earlier eras, Zambia had large stands of teak, mahogany, and other valuable hardwood trees. Loggers cut down most of these trees in the twentieth century. Some companies continue to log and export hardwoods, which are prized worldwide for making furniture, floors, paneling, and other products. However, most of the wood cut down in Zambia remains in Zambia. People build with it and burn it for heating and cooking.

The Informal Sector

Many Zambian workers make their living in the "informal economy"—a vast network of people without regular, legal, or full-time employment. This network includes street vendors, who sell fruit, nuts, clothing, and household goods in urban shantytowns. It includes people engaged in illegal activities, such as drug dealing and prostitution. It also includes businesses that operate without government permission or oversight. Such businesses often ignore workplace safety rules. They often pay substandard wages.

Many children work in Zambia—in both formal and informal jobs. Some child workers are AIDS orphans who must work because they have no parents to support them. Other child workers have parents, but their families are so desperately poor that even the children must work. Children as young as four sometimes work at dangerous jobs at Zambian mines, factories, farms, and construction sites. Some work as street vendors, trash haulers, or servants. Some girls work as prostitutes. Other children simply beg on the streets. Zambia has laws against child labor, but these laws are largely ignored.

Transportation

A network of roadways links Zambia's major cities. These roads total about 56,500 miles (91,000 km) in length. Only about 12,500 miles (20,000 km) are paved roads. The rest are dirt roads, which quickly turn to mud in the rainy season.

A railroad line runs from Livingstone in the south to Ndola in the north. At the city of Kapiri Mposhi, another rail line runs east to Tunduma and the Tanzanian border. Zambia's railroads are mainly used for transporting industrial products rather than passengers.

Most Zambians who travel from city to city take buses. Most of the buses are old and poorly maintained. Bus trips, even between not distant cities, can turn into long ordeals when buses break down along the way.

Zambia has nine airports with paved runways. Lusaka has an international airport, with flights to Great Britain, India, and

THE CHINA SYNDROME

Since the 1970s, Zambia has had strong relations with China. Chinese companies have built factories and textile mills in Zambia. They have invested in copper and other mines. The Chinese government has helped Zambia build roads, railroads, hospitals, and schools. It has given Zambia millions of dollars in aid money. Zambia imports many Chinese-made products, including machinery, clothing, and household goods. Small numbers of Chinese work in Zambia. Most of them are temporary workers on construction projects. But some Chinese have come to stay. They have bought homes and opened up shops in Zambian cities. Zambians can even eat Chinese food in Lusaka.

LIGHTS OUT

Zambia uses its rushing rivers to generate hydroelectric power. But the nation is too poor to build power stations and electrical lines for all its homes and businesses. Only 20 percent of Zambian homes have electrical power. Most of them are in cities. In rural areas, only 3 percent of households have electricity. Even people with electricity often experience blackouts—times when the power grid fails and all the lights go out. During those times, people rely on generators and batteries to provide power, or they simply do without electricity.

surrounding African nations. Zambia Airways is the nation's main airline, with both national and international flights. Smaller airlines run flights between some Zambian cities. About one hundred cities have unpaved fields used for takeoffs and landings.

Commercial ferries take travelers across Lake Kariba, Lake Tanganyika, and the Zambezi River. Zambia has a shipping port at Mpulungu, at the southern tip of Lake Tanganyika. Fishers, rafters, kayakers, and other sportspeople sometimes paddle on Zambia's rivers in small craft. Sightseeing boats also cruise the Zambezi and other rivers. But because of waterfalls and strong rapids, Zambia's rivers are not suitable for cargo ships.

A ferry transports passengers across Lake Tanganyika.

Communications

In theory, Zambians enjoy freedom of the press. However, the state owns most of the nation's TV stations and newspapers. This situation gives the news a progovernment slant. Private news organizations are allowed to operate without restrictions, although they frequently suffer from a lack of money.

Zambia has nine television stations, which broadcast sports, news, soap operas, religious shows, and movies. Viewers with satellite television can also watch stations from South Africa, Great Britain, and the United States. More than twenty Zambian radio stations offer a variety of music, news, and talk shows. Radio and TV stations broadcast in English as well as indigenous languages.

Zambia has about 100,000 computer users, mostly concentrated in Lusaka and other cities. About 95,000 Zambian homes have land-line telephones. Another 950,000 Zambians use cell phones.

The Zambian government publishes two daily English-language newspapers: the *Times of Zambia* and the *Zambia Daily Mail*. Private English-language newspapers include the *Post*, the *National Mirror*, the *Monitor*, *Today*, and the *Star*. Indigenous-language newspapers are also available throughout the country.

The Future

Zambia's future is uncertain. The AIDS crisis has devastated the adult population. The disease has harmed the Zambian workforce, the children of people with AIDS, social traditions, and family life. Because of AIDS and other illnesses, most Zambians will not live to old age.

A foreign aid worker helps an **AIDS patient** in a hospice in Zambia.

Zambia is becoming a nation of young people who can no longer look to their parents, grandparents, and other elders for guidance and support.

The Zambian government, with the help of international organizations, is working to fight AIDS, poverty, and hunger. Programs include building wells for clean water, building schools and health clinics, distributing vaccines, and paying for medicines to treat people with AIDS and other illnesses. Every year, foreign governments and agencies contribute around $500 million in aid to Zambia.

Some positive economic trends began in 2005. First, the World Bank wrote off $3.8 billion in Zambian debt—loans that the government had been struggling to repay. The debt relief has freed up money for Zambia to spend on health care, education, and other social services. Also in 2005, world copper prices began to rise. Higher copper prices translate into more jobs for Zambian mine workers. In 2006 exploration teams discovered oil and gas in western Zambia. President Mwanawasa has invited energy companies to explore the reserves. A new business in oil and gas could be an economic boon for Zambia. Meanwhile, tourism continues to increase, with jobs and money arriving in Zambia along with the tourists.

TOURIST MAGNET

Victoria Falls is one of the biggest tourist attractions in Africa. Hundreds of thousands of people visit the falls each year. Some fly over the falls in ultralight airplanes *(below)*. Others raft down the white-water rapids beneath the falls. On sunny days, rainbows float in the spray above the falls. When the moon is full, tourists can even see moonbows, created by moonlight shining through the spray.

Even with these positive trends, Zambia faces an uphill battle against poverty, hunger, and disease. Zambians have overcome many problems in the past. In the 1950s and 1960s, they organized politically to win independence from the British. In the following years, they melded a diverse group of people into a peaceful and unified nation. When their leaders tried to take too much power, Zambians said no. They demanded new leaders and democratic elections. It's clear that despite the obstacles they face, Zambians will not give up without a fight. They will continue to work together to create a better nation and a better future.

Prehistory   Early human beings live in Zambia.

CA. 500 B.C.   Migrants from the north introduce iron making, farming, and livestock herding to Zambia.

CA. A.D. 600   Zambian villagers begin to trade with one another.

CA. 1100   Arab traders come to Zambia to obtain ivory, gold, and copper. They enslave local inhabitants.

Late 1400s   Portuguese explorers arrive in Africa.

Late 1700s   European missionaries begin to travel to Africa to teach people about Christianity.

1855   Scottish missionary and explorer David Livingstone becomes the first European to see Victoria Falls.

1889   Cecil Rhodes claims Zambia as a British territory, to be run by his British South Africa Company. He names the territory Northern Rhodesia.

1911   Livingstone becomes the capital of Northern Rhodesia.

1914-1918   The British draft twenty thousand Northern Rhodesian men to serve as laborers during World War I.

1921   Miners discover the remains of Broken Hill Man. The bones are between 125,000 and 300,000 years old.

1924   The British Colonial Office takes control of Northern Rhodesia.

1928   British colonists discover vast reserves of copper in Northern Rhodesia.

1935   The Northern Rhodesian capital moves from Livingstone to Lusaka.

1939-1945   Northern Rhodesian men serve in the British military during World War II.

1948   Indigenous welfare associations merge to form the Northern Rhodesian Congress.

1949   Miners band together to form the Northern Rhodesia African Mineworkers Union.

1953   Northern Rhodesia, Southern Rhodesia, and Nyasaland merge into a state called the Central African Federation.

1958   Indigenous leaders form the Zambia African National Congress. Engineers dam the Zambezi River, creating Lake Kariba in southern Zambia.

1960   British prime minister Harold Macmillan gives his "wind of change" speech about African independence.

1964   Zambia becomes an independent republic.

1966   The University of Zambia opens in Lusaka.

1969   The Zambian government buys a controlling share in the nation's copper mines.

Early 1970s   The price of copper falls, damaging Zambia's economy.

1973   The United National Independence Party (UNIP) becomes the only legal party in Zambia.

1975   UNIP takes over Zambia's biggest newspapers.

1976   Engineers dam the Kafue River, creating Lake Itezhi-Tezhi.

Mid-1980s   The AIDS epidemic begins to sweep through Zambia.

1991   In national elections, the Movement for a Multiparty Democracy defeats President Kenneth Kaunda and the UNIP. Frederick Chiluba becomes Zambia's new president.

1996   Zambian hurdler Samuel Matete wins a silver medal at the Summer Olympic Games.

Early 2000s   Zambia suffers severe droughts, leading to widespread hunger.

2001   Levy Mwanawasa becomes president of Zambia.

2005   The World Bank writes off more than 50 percent of Zambia's foreign debt. Malama Katulwende publishes *Bitterness*, a novel about modern Zambia.

2006   Golfer Madalitso Muthiya plays in the U.S. Open golf tournament.

2008   Energy companies begin large-scale oil and gas exploration in Zambia.

COUNTRY NAME: Republic of Zambia

AREA: 290,585 square miles (752,615 sq. km)

MAIN LANDFORMS: Kayamba Hills, Mafinga Hills, Mbala Highlands, Muchinga Mountains, Mufulwe Hills, Tonga Plateau, Victoria Falls, Zambezi Escarpment

HIGHEST POINT: Unnamed peak in the Mafinga Hills (7,549 ft. or 2,301 m)

LOWEST POINT: Zambezi River (1,085 ft. or 329 m)

MAJOR RIVERS: Chambeshi, Kafue, Luangwa, Zambezi

ANIMALS: African buffalo, antelopes, baboons, cheetahs, crocodiles, elephants, eagles, giraffes, hippopotamuses, hyenas, leopards, lions, lizards, monkeys, snakes, zebras

CAPITAL CITY: Lusaka

OTHER MAJOR CITIES: Kitwe, Livingstone, Ndola

OFFICIAL LANGUAGE: English

MONETARY UNIT: Kwacha. 1 kwacha = 100 ngwee

CURRENCY

Zambia uses a unit of currency called the kwacha. The name *kwacha* means "dawn" in the Bemba language. The name is a reference to the slogan "a new dawn of freedom," which was popular during the fight for independence.

One kwacha is not worth very much. In January 2008, it took 3,735 kwacha to equal just one U.S. dollar. The Zambian government issues paper money in denominations of 20, 50, 100, 500, 5,000, and 10,000 kwacha. It issues 1-, 5-, and 10-kwacha coins. The kwacha is divided into 100 ngwee. The government issues 25- and 50-ngwee coins, but people rarely use them, since they are worth so little.

The Zambian flag has a green background with three vertical stripes in the bottom right-hand corner. A fish eagle—Zambia's national bird flies above the stripes. The stripes are red, black, and orange.

The eagle symbolizes Zambians' ability to rise above their problems. The colors on the flag also have meanings. Red stands for the nation's struggle for freedom. Black symbolizes Zambia's people. Orange represents its mineral wealth, especially copper. The green background stands for Zambia's natural resources. Zambia adopted the flag upon independence in 1964.

Zambia's national anthem is "Stand and Sing of Zambia, Proud and Free." The anthem is an adaptation of the song "Nkosɪ Sɪkelel' ɪAfrika" (God Bless Africa), written around the turn of the twentieth century by Enoch Mankayi Sontonga, a South African teacher. In 1964 leaders of the newly independent Zambia changed the words to fit their nation. Zambians sometimes sing the anthem in Bemba. Here is the first verse and chorus in English:

> Stand and sing of Zambia, proud and free,
> Land of work and joy in unity,
> Victors in the struggle for the right,
> We have won freedom's fight.
> All one, strong and free.

> Praise be to God.
> Praise be, praise be, praise be,
> Bless our great nation,
> Zambia, Zambia, Zambia.
> Free men we stand
> Under the flag of our land.
> Zambia, praise to thee!
> All one, strong and free.

To hear the melody and read the complete English lyrics as well as the Bemba lyrics of Zambia's national anthem, visit www.vgsbooks.com for links.

MALAMA KATULWENDE (b. 1967) Katulwende has earned acclaim as a poet and novelist. He was born in Zambia's Luapula Province. As a young man, he attended the University of Zambia and later taught math and science to Zambian schoolchildren. Katulwende's poems have appeared in the anthology *Under the African Skies: Poetry from Zambia* (2001). In 2005 he published his first novel, *Bitterness*. The novel examines the tension between ancient traditions and modern life in Zambia.

DAVID LIVINGSTONE (1813–1873). Missionary-turned-explorer David Livingstone was born in Blantyre, Scotland. He studied medicine at the University of Glasgow, but his true passion was religion. He wanted to help spread Christianity around the globe. He also wanted to end the African slave trade and open up the African interior to European commerce. The London Missionary Society sent Livingstone to southern Africa in the 1850s. He undertook a series of expeditions, including crossing Africa from coast to coast between 1853 and 1856. During this journey, he was the first European to see Victoria Falls. While searching for the source of the Nile River, Livingstone died in Zambia in 1873. The city of Livingstone is named in his honor.

ROZALLA MILLER (b. 1964) Known by her first name, Rozalla is a favorite of rave and club-dance music fans. She was born in Ndola but moved to Zimbabwe as a teenager. In Zimbabwe she began singing with a local band. In the late 1980s, she moved to London to further her career. Her first album, *Everybody's Free*, came out in 1991. It included a worldwide dance hit, "Everybody's Free (to Feel Good)." In 1992 Rozalla toured with U.S. superstar Michael Jackson on his *Dangerous* tour. Afterward, she continued to record dance music. Her song "I Love Music" served as the soundtrack for the 1993 Hollywood movie *Carlito's Way*. After making dance music for more than fifteen years, in 2007 Rozalla started work on a more soul- and jazz-oriented album.

MADALITSO MUTHIYA (b. 1983) Muthiya, a professional golfer, was born into a middle-class family in Lusaka. As a boy, he was passionate about soccer. But his father played golf, and Muthiya grew curious about the sport. He began to play with a set of mismatched clubs. He perfected his swing by watching U.S. and British golf tournaments on satellite television. When Muthiya was fifteen, his father arranged for him to enter a junior golf tournament in Florida. There, he caught the eye of the golf coach from the University of New Mexico. The coach arranged for Muthiya to attend the university on a scholarship. After graduating, Muthiya joined the Canadian professional golf tour. In 2006, at the age of twenty-three, he played (but scored poorly) in the U.S. Open, the most famous U.S. golf tournament.

LEVY MWANAWASA (b. 1948) Mwanawasa, Zambia's third president, was born in Mufulira. As a young man, he attended the University of Zambia, where he earned a law degree. He practiced law privately from 1974 to 1978. He then took a job as a lawyer with the Zambian government. He served as the nation's vice president from 1991 to 1994 and then returned to his private law practice. In 2001 he won the nation's presidential election. He was reelected in 2006. During his presidency, Mwanawasa has fought to rid the Zambian government of corruption and has worked with international agencies to improve Zambia's economy.

AMON SIMUTOWE (b. 1982) Simutowe is a champion chess player. He was born in Ndola. When Simutowe was ten, his older brother taught him to play chess. At the age of twelve, he began to enter local chess tournaments. In 1995 he won Zambia's national championship for players under twenty-one. He was only thirteen at the time. One year later, he won Zambia's national adult championship. After that, Simutowe made a steady rise through world chess competition. He earned the rank of international master at the age of sixteen. In 2002 Simutowe won a scholarship to study at the University of Texas at Dallas. While in school, he played for the university's chess team. He graduated in 2006 with a degree in finance and economics. In 2007 Simutowe became a grand master, the highest ranking in chess.

FRIDAY TEMBO (1962–2004) Tembo, a native of Lusaka, earned fame as a sculptor. He had no formal art training and worked for many years as a copper miner. In 1987 he began making and exhibiting sculpture. He developed a distinctive style, with carved wood and metal figures inspired by traditional Zambian artwork. Throughout the 1990s, Tembo exhibited his works in Africa as well as Europe. His pieces won many awards. In the years before his death, Tembo passed on his knowledge to a group of young apprentice artists, who worked for him in his studio.

PRINCESS KASUNE ZULU (b. 1977) A native of Kabwe, Zulu is a prominent international AIDS activist. She was just a girl when AIDS swept though southern Africa. First, her infant sister died of AIDS and then her mother. Next, her father grew sick. He died in 1994, when Zulu was seventeen. Zulu took an HIV test and learned that she was infected with the AIDS virus. At that point, she dedicated herself to becoming an AIDS educator and activist. Working with a group called the Hope Initiative, she is teaching Zambians about HIV prevention and is running support groups for people with HIV/AIDS. In the late 1990s, Zulu began taking her message to an international audience. She spoke to the United Nations and world leaders. She began a radio show, *Positive Living*, which is broadcast throughout Zambia. Many U.S. magazines and newspapers have reported on Zulu's work. She has won numerous awards from AIDS and human-rights organizations.

KAFUE NATIONAL PARK This park in western Zambia provides a home for antelope, lions, leopards, spotted hyenas, elephants, African buffalo, and hundreds of bird species. Travelers come from all over the world to view the animals in their natural surroundings.

LAKE BANGWEULU The lake and surrounding wetlands provide a home for hundreds of bird species, including egrets, herons, ducks, storks, geese, gulls, plovers, pelicans, and flamingos. Lucky bird-watchers might also catch a glimpse of the shoebill stork, one of the world's rarest birds.

LAKE TANGANYIKA Zambia borders the southernmost tip of Lake Tanganyika at the Tanzanian border. Here, visitors can fish, snorkel, and bird-watch. Nearby are the Kalambo Falls, the second-highest waterfall in Africa—about double the height of Victoria Falls. Archaeologists have found evidence that Stone Age peoples lived in this area as early as three hundred thousand years ago.

LIVINGSTONE MEMORIAL A plain stone monument marks the place where British explorer David Livingstone died in the village of Chitambo in 1873. His followers buried his heart and other internal organs under a tree that once stood here. They shipped the rest of his body back to London, where it was buried in Westminster Abbey, a famous church.

LUSAKA NATIONAL MUSEUM This museum in Zambia's capital city offers exhibits on Zambian culture and history. Visitors will see works by contemporary Zambian painters and sculptors, traditional Zambian crafts and instruments, history exhibits, and a cast, or replica, of Broken Hill Man, the famous prehistoric skeleton.

OLD SLAVE TREE This old mahogany tree sits on Makoli Avenue in the city of Ndola. The tree was once a meeting place for East African slave traders. British administrators outlawed slave trading in Zambia in the 1800s. A plaque at the foot of the tree commemorates this event.

SHIWA NG'ANDU British colonist Stewart Gore-Browne built this settlement in northeastern Zambia in the 1920s. The highlight is a magnificent brick manor house, filled with exquisite wooden furniture, silver ornaments, and a vast library. The estate is the most distinctive remnant of Zambia's British colonial era.

VICTORIA FALLS This giant waterfall on the Zambezi River is one of the Seven Natural Wonders of the World. At the falls, the Zambezi is more than 1 mile (1.6 km) wide. It plunges over a 350-foot (107 m) cliff into a gorge below. Visitors can see rainbows, moonbows, and other breathtaking sights above, beneath, and near the falls.

animist religion: a religion that involves belief in spirits, including the spirits of animals, bodies of water, natural events (such as storms and lightning), and human ancestors

colony: a territory governed by a distant nation and sometimes inhabited by settlers from that nation

corruption: widespread dishonesty, bribery, and other illegal activity within a government, business, or other organization

drought: a long period without rain, during which crops wither or won't grow

epidemic: a widespread outbreak of disease

hunter-gatherers: people who obtain food by hunting, fishing, trapping, and gathering wild plants rather than by farming or raising animals

hydroelectric power: electricity produced by the power of rushing water. People often dam rivers to create hydroelectric power stations.

indigenous: native to a particular place. Indigenous people are those whose ancestors were among the earliest inhabitants of a specific place.

migrant laborer: a person who leaves his or her home or moves regularly to find work

missionary: a religious teacher who tries to convert others to his or her faith

nationalism: a philosophy that emphasizes loyalty to one's own nation above all else. Nationalist goals often include independence from foreign rule.

refugee: a person who flees his or her country to escape danger or persecution

subsistence farming: growing only enough crops to feed one's family, with little or nothing left over to sell

Western: European or North American in outlook, culture, and social organization

Baylies, Carolyn, and Janet Bujra, eds. *AIDS, Sexuality and Gender in Africa: Collective Strategies and Struggles in Tanzania and Zambia*. London: Routledge, 2000.
In this scholarly work, a group of experts explores the AIDS epidemic in Tanzania and Zambia. The writers examine the social dynamics that put women in these nations at a high risk for HIV infection and propose strategies for empowering women in the fight against HIV and AIDS.

BBC. "Country Profile: Zambia." *BBC News*. September 20, 2007.
http://news.bbc.co.uk/1/hi/world/africa/country_profiles/1069294.stm (December 2007).
This website, created by the British Broadcasting Corporation, offers an excellent overview of modern Zambia. This site offers links to news articles about Zambia, as well as additional recommended websites.

Central Intelligence Agency. "Zambia." *The World Factbook*. December 13, 2007.
https://www.cia.gov/library/publications/the-world-factbook/geos/za.html (December 2007).
This Web resource offers facts and statistics on Zambia's geography, people, government, economy, and infrastructure.

Jeal, Tim. *Livingstone*. New York: G. P. Putnam's Sons, 1973.
This riveting biography shows how David Livingstone obsessively traveled through southern Africa, determined to combat slavery, spread Christianity, open up the region to European trade, and find the source of the Nile River. Jeal examines both the myths and the realities surrounding this famous explorer.

Jordán, Manuel. *Makishi: Mask Characters of Zambia*. Los Angeles: Fowler Museum at UCLA, 2006.
Makishi masks worn by dancers in northwestern Zambia are at once stunning, frightening, and fascinating. This book includes dozens of full-color photographs of masks, dancers, and Makishi costumes. The accompanying text explains the mask characters and the meaning of the dances.

Kaplan, Irving, ed. *Zambia: A Country Study*. Washington, DC: American University, 1979.
This book offers excellent examinations of Zambia's landscape and history. It also includes sections on Zambian culture, society, economy, and government, although some of this material is outdated.

McIntyre, Chris. *Zambia: The Bradt Travel Guide*. Chalfont St. Peter, UK: Bradt Travel Guides, 2004.
This travel guidebook offers extensive information about Zambia's landscape, animals, history, and culture. It also details Zambia's sightseeing highlights and provides practical facts for travelers.

Musambachime, Mwelwa. *Basic Facts on Zambia*. Bloomington, IN: Author House, 2005.
The author, Zambia's former ambassador to the United Nations, offers a thorough overview of his home country. He details the nation's history, geography, plant and animal life, economy, and culture.

Swiller, Josh. *The Unheard: A Memoir of Deafness and Africa.* **New York: Henry Holt and Company, 2007.**
Swiller, a deaf man, spent two years in Zambia as a Peace Corps volunteer. He recounts his experiences in a small Zambian village and describes how life in Zambia gave him new insight into his own deafness.

Thomas, Antony. *Rhodes: The Race for Africa.* **New York: St. Martin's Press, 1996.**
Englishman Cecil Rhodes used ruthlessness and business savvy to conquer much of southern and central Africa, including lands that would become Zambia. This biography describes his life and conquests.

Turner, Barry, ed. *The Statesman's Yearbook 2007: The Politics, Cultures and Economies of the World.* **New York: Palgrave Macmillan, 2006.**
This reference book offers at-a-glance summaries of nations around the world. Topics include history, climate, government, economy, international relations, communications, education, and culture.

U.S. Department of State, "Background Note: Zambia." *State.gov.* **December 2007.**
 http://www.state.gov/r/pa/ei/bgn/2359.htm (December 2007).
This Web reference lists facts and statistics about Zambia's people, government, and economy. It also includes discussions on the nation's history and current political situation.

Cornell, Kari. *Cooking the Southern African Way.* **Minneapolis: Lerner Publications Company, 2005.**
This book offers easy-to-follow recipes from the nations of southern Africa, including Zambia. Readers will also learn about history and culture in Zambia and neighboring nations.

Crocodiles!
http://www.pbs.org/wgbh/nova/crocs/
Crocodiles make their homes in Zambia's rivers, lakes, and swamps. But these animals are threatened by illegal hunting. This website, a companion to a *NOVA* television program of the same name, sheds light on these fascinating animals.

DiPiazza, Francesca. *Zimbabwe in Pictures.* **Minneapolis: Twenty-First Century Books, 2005.**
Zambia and Zimbabwe share a border as well as a common history. Both nations were once British colonies named for Cecil Rhodes. Both share the glorious Victoria Falls, one of the world's seven natural wonders. And both nations struggle with AIDS, poverty, and other hardships. This book examines Zambia's southern neighbor in great detail.

Embassy of the Republic of Zambia
http://www.zambiaembassy.org
Visit this website for information on Zambian culture, government, and economy, as well as practical information for visitors to Zambia.

Holmes, Timothy. *Zambia.* **New York: Benchmark Books, 1998.**
This book offers an overview of Zambia's geography, history, economy, and culture. Full-color photographs help bring the text to life.

Markle, Sandra. *Termites.* **Minneapolis: Lerner Publications Company, 2007.**
The Zambian countryside is dotted with termite towers. What are termites and why do they build towers? Find out in this photo- and fact-filled book.

Mosi-oa-Tunya/Victoria Falls
http://whc.unesco.org/en/list/509
In 1989 the United Nations Educational, Scientific, and Cultural Organization named Victoria Falls a World Heritage Site—a treasure to be protected for future generations. This Web page gives basic facts about the falls and provides links to information on other World Heritage Sites.

Poole, Joyce. *Elephants.* **Stillwater, MN: Voyager Press, 1997.**
Zambia has established nineteen national parks to protect elephants and other animals. This book describes elephants in great detail. Lush color photographs accompany the text.

Storad, Conrad. *Inside AIDS: HIV Attacks the Immune System.* **Minneapolis: Twenty-First Century Books, 1998.**
Zambia has one of the highest rates of HIV infection in the world. This book explains HIV and AIDS from a medical viewpoint. It describes how HIV attacks the human immune system and tells what researchers and doctors are doing to fight the virus.

vgsbooks.com
http://www.vgsbooks.com

Visit vgsbooks.com, the homepage of the Visual Geography Series®. You can get linked to all sorts of useful online information, including geographical, historical, demographic, cultural, and economic websites. The vgsbooks.com site is a great resource for late-breaking news and statistics.

Worth, Richard. *Stanley and Livingstone and the Exploration of Africa in World History.* Berkeley Heights, NJ: Enslow Publishers, 2000.

Explorer David Livingstone left his mark on Zambia in several ways. He named Victoria Falls, explored the Zambezi River, and paved the way for European colonization in south central Africa. When Livingstone went missing in the African wilderness, explorer Henry Stanley came to find him. This book tells both men's stories.

Zambia
http://www.zambiatourism.com

This website offers a comprehensive overview of Zambia and its attractions. In addition to information for travelers, the site includes pages on Zambia's history, culture, and environment.

African independence movement, 29, 30
agricultural practices, 17, 36–37, 59–60
AIDS epidemic, 7, 32, 41–42, 63–64. *See also* health issues
Angola, 8
Arab traders, 4, 23, 24, 47
arts, fine, 51–52

Bangweulu, Lake, 12, 72
Bemba ethnic group, 35
Botswana, 8
British Colonial Office, 26–27, 29
British South Africa Company (BSAC), 25–26
Broken Hill Man, 22

Central African Federation, 29, 30
Chambeshi River, 11
Chiluba, Frederick, 31–32
China, 61
Christianity, spread of, 24–25, 26, 27, 46–47
cities, 18–19, 37–38
climate, 12–14
colonization, 4–5, 25–30
communications and media, 63
copper deposits, 5, 7, 16, 27. *See also* mining industry
crafts and fine art, 51–52
cultural life, traditional, 7
currency, 68

dance, 49–51
debt relief, 64
Democratic Republic of Congo, 8
dress and attire, 36
drought, 17, 40

economy: agricultural practices, 59–60; communications and media, 63; future, 63–65; after independence, 31, 32; industry, 57–58; service sector, 56–57; transportation, 61–62
education, 42–43
environmental problems, 17–18
ethnic groups, 34–35
European colonization, 4–5, 24–30

fauna, 15–16
festivals, 48
fish eagle, 7, 15
flag, 69
flora, 14–15
food and cooking, 52–53

geography, 8–12
government system, 32–33
Great Britain, 5, 25–30

health issues, 39–40. *See also* AIDS epidemic
Hinduism, 47
history: independence, 5–7, 29–31; modern, 31–33; prehistory, 4–5, 20–23
holidays and festivals, 48
Homo erectus, 20
Homo sapiens, 20
hydroelectric power, 17, 62

ifisashi sauce, 53
independence, 5–7, 29–31
indigenous chiefs, 27
indigenous religions, 47
industry, 57–58
Iron Age, 21–23
Islam, 47
isolo, 55
Itezhi-Tezhi, Lake, 12

judicial system, 33

Kafue National Park, 12, 18, 72
Kafue river, 9
Kariba, Lake, 12, 62
Katulwende, Malama, 46, 70
Kaunda, Kenneth, 7, 31
Kayamba Hills, 9
Kitwe, Zambia, 19
Ku-omboka ceremony, 48, 49

lakes, 12
language groups, 34–36
literacy, 43
literature, 44–46
Livingstone, David, 24–25, 70
Livingstone, Zambia, 11, 19
Livingstone Memorial, 72

Index

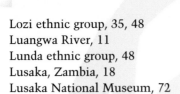
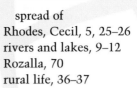

Lozi ethnic group, 35, 48
Luangwa River, 11
Lunda ethnic group, 48
Lusaka, Zambia, 18
Lusaka National Museum, 72

Macmillan, Harold, 29, 30
Mafinga Hills, 9
Makishi dancers, 50
malaria, 39
Malawi, 8, 29
Mansa, Zambia, 12
maps, 6, 10
Mbala Highlands, 9
Miller, Rozalla, 70
mineral resources, 7, 16, 57–58
mining industry, 7, 17, 27–28, 57–58
missionaries, Christian, 24–25, 26, 27
Movement for Multiparty Democracy, 31
Mozambique, 8
Muchinga Mountains, 9
Mufulwe Hills, 9
music and dance, 49–51
Muthiya, Madalitso, 54, 70
Mwanawasa, Levy, 32, 71
Mweru, Lake, 12
Mweru Wantipa, Lake, 12

Namibia, 8
national anthem, 69
National Assembly, 32–33
nationalism, 30
national parks, 18
natural resources, 16–17
Ndola, Zambia, 18–19
Northern Rhodesia, 25–26, 30
Northern Rhodesia Congress, 28
Nsenga ethnic group, 36
nshima, 52
Nyanja language, 36
Nyasaland, 29

Old Slave Tree, 72

poaching, 18
population, 34
provinces, 33
religion, 46–47. See also Christianity,

spread of
Rhodes, Cecil, 5, 25–26
rivers and lakes, 9–12
Rozalla, 70
rural life, 36–37

settlers, white, 28–29
Shiwa Ng'andu, 72
Sifuniso, Monde, 46
Simutowe, Amon, 71
Sinyangwe, Binwell, 46
slavery, 4, 24
Southern Rhodesia, 25–26
sports and recreation, 53–55
Stone Age, 20–21

Tanganyika, Lake, 12, 62, 72
Tanzania, 8
Tembo, Friday, 71
termites, 16
terrain and geography, 8–12
Tonga ethnic group, 11, 35
Tonga Plateau, 9
tourism, 18, 32, 56–57, 64
trade, 22–23, 24
transportation, 61–62
Tumbuka ethnic group, 35–36

United National Independence Party, 30, 31
University of Zambia, 31, 43
urban life, 37–38

Victoria Falls, 11, 12, 64, 72
village life, 36–37

water supply issues, 39
women's rights, 43
World War I, 26
World War II, 27–28

Zambezi Escarpment, 9
Zambezi River, 11, 62
Zambian African National Congress, 29–30
Zimbabwe, 8, 25
Zulu, Princess Kasune, 71

Captions for photos appearing on cover and chapter openers:

Cover: This aerial view of Victoria Falls shows the width of the river and the depth of the chasm that creates the falls.

pp. 4–5 Lusaka is the capital city of Zambia.

pp. 8–9 The Zambezi River flows through western and southern Zambia.

pp. 34–35 Men and women sell fresh vegetables at a market in northeastern Zambia.

pp. 44–45 A man performs a traditional dance in South Luangwa National Park.

pp. 56–57 Tourists ride elephants through the Zambian countryside.

Photo Acknowledgments

The images in this book are used with the permission of: © Ian Murphy/ Stone/Getty Images, pp. 4–5; © XNR Productions, pp. 6, 10; © Richard du Toit/Gallo Images ROOTS RF collection/Getty Images, pp. 8–9; © Frans Lemmens/The Image Bank/Getty Images, p. 11; © Jorgen Schytte/Peter Arnold, Inc., p. 13; © Images of Africa Photobank/Alamy, p. 14; © Gerald Hoberman/drr.net, p. 15; © G P Bowater/Alamy, p. 16; © Liba Taylor/Panos Pictures, p. 19; © akg-images, p. 22; © Welgos/Hulton Archive/Getty Images, p. 23; Library of Congress (LC-USZ62-16529), p. 24; © North Wind Picture Archives, p. 25; © Bettmann/CORBIS, p. 28; © Central Press/Hulton Archive/ Getty Images, p. 30; © Terrence Spencer/Time & Life Pictures/Getty Images, p. 31; © Emmanuel Dunand/AFP/Getty Images, p. 32; © Sue Cunningham Photographic/Alamy, pp. 34–35, 62; © Joan Wakelin/Art Directors, p. 37; © Nikos Kokkas/drr.net, p. 38; AP Photo/Obed Zilwa, p. 40; © David Bratley/Alamy, pp. 41, 46; © Constantia Treppe/Art Directors, pp. 42, 47, 52; © Michael Beard/Art Directors, pp. 44–45; © JTB Photo Communications, Inc./Alamy, p. 49; © Nick Graves/Alamy, p. 50; © Cindy Miller Hopkins/ drr.net, p. 51; © Lefty Shivambu/Gallo Images/Getty Images, p. 54; © Annie Griffiths Belt/National Geographic/Getty Images, pp. 56–57; © Martin Norris/ Alamy, p. 58; © Sean Sprague/Alamy, p. 59; © age fotostock/SuperStock, p. 60; © Tom Stoddard Archive/Getty Images, p. 63; © Travel Ink/Gallo Images/ Getty Images, p. 64; Audrius Tomonis—www.banknotes.com, p. 68; © Laura Westlund/Independent Picture Service, p. 69.

Front cover: © Chris Sattlberger/The Image Bank/Getty Images.
Back cover: NASA.